Perennial
Gardening
with
Derek Fell

Perennial Gardening

with

Derek Fell

*Practical Advice and
Personal Favorites
from the Best Selling Author
and Television Show Host*

FRIEDMAN/FAIRFAX
PUBLISHERS

A FRIEDMAN/FAIRFAX BOOK

Library of Congress Cataloging-in-Publication Data

Fell, Derek.
    Perennial gardening with Derek Fell / written and photographed
by Derek Fell
        p.   cm.
    Includes index.
    ISBN 1-56799-252-8 (hardcover)
    1. Perennials.   2. Landscape gardening.   I. Title.
SB434.F455   1996
635.9'32—dc20   95-49634
                                                            CIP

Editor: Susan Lauzau
Art Director: Jeff Batzli
Designer: Susan Livingston
Photography Director: Christopher C. Bain
Production Associate: Marnie Ann Boardman

Color separations by Bright Arts (Singapore) Pte Ltd.
Printed in the United Kingdom by Butler & Tanner, Ltd.

For bulk purchases and special sales, please contact:
Friedman/Fairfax Publishers
Attention: Sales Department
15 West 26th Street
New York, NY 10010
212/685-6610   FAX 212/685-1307

Frontispiece: Perfect partners—Rudbeckia hirta and 'Red Magic' daylilies.

Dedication

For my three children, Christina, Victoria, and Derek Jr.,
all of whom love gardening.

Acknowledgments

It was the late Jan de Graaff, Oregon lily hybridizer, who introduced me to the wonderful world of hardy perennials. Through his European distributors I helped introduce his wonderful strains of hybrid lilies to Great Britain and other European countries—varieties like the remarkable giant-flowered 'Imperial' strain, the vigorous 'Mid-Century' hybrids, including 'Enchantment' , and the classic trumpet lily 'Black Dragon'.

I also owe my love of perennials to other great American plant breeders, who I met after moving to North America—people such as Paul Aden, of hosta breeding fame; Kurt Bleumel, ornamental grass specialist; Arthur Kroll, daylily expert, and Al Russell, leading wholesale grower, who allows me free reign of his farm to photograph perennials in all seasons. I am also indebted to the experts at Spring Hill Nurseries, whose extensive test gardens at Tipp City, Ohio, have proven invaluable in appraising newer varieties.

In recent years I have greatly enjoyed planning and planting one of North America's largest perennial gardens—in a series of twenty-five theme gardens at my home, historic Cedaridge Farm, in Bucks County, Pennsylvania. None of this planting, however, would have been possible without the help of my grounds supervisor, Wendy Fields, and my wife, Carolyn (who herself owned a 64-acre cut flower farm in upstate New York before we were married).

Thanks also to Kathy Nelson, my office manager, who helps to keep my extensive photo library organized.

Contents

Opposite: Spires of pink Russell hybrid lupines contrast beautifully against barn siding.

Bearded irises massed along a streamside create a stunning floral display.

Introduction

You may wonder what qualifies me to write about perennials. First, I am told that my home, Cedaridge Farm, is one of the most inspirational perennial gardens in North America. Featured in *Architectural Digest, Gardens Illustrated, American Nurseryman,* and *Beautiful Gardens* magazines, and visited by thousands of gardeners every year, the gardens at Cedaridge Farm have won awards from the Pennsylvania Horticultural Society and from other landscape design associations. A series of twenty-five theme gardens features extensive collections of lilies, peonies, daylilies, hostas, primulas, irises, ferns, and ornamental grasses, as well as other perennial plants.

For many years I have supplied perennial garden designs and photography to North America's biggest perennial plant nursery, Spring Hill Nurseries, showing beginning gardeners how to plant all kinds of small-space perennial gardens from mailbox and patio surrounds to sunny beds and shady corners.

With my wife, Carolyn, I have also coauthored one of North America's best-selling perennial books, *550 Perennial Garden Ideas*. This volume, which represents twenty-five years of documenting perennial gardens, sold more than thirty thousand copies in its first year. *Ornamental Grass Gardening* won a best photography award from the Garden Writers Association of America, and was followed by *The Ornamental Grass Gardening Encyclopedia*, which involved photography in perennial gardens from coast to coast. My *Step-by-Step Gardening* television show for the QVC cable shopping channel is one of the nation's most highly rated gardening shows, and primarily features collections of perennial plants.

In recent years perennial gardening has burgeoned into one of the hottest gardening activities, but with that interest has come a great deal of confusion and misinformation. In this book, you'll learn how to select the best perennials for your situation, which is the key to growing beautiful, healthy plants.

Perhaps the overriding reason to grow perennials is their tenacity and ability to come back year after year without replanting and, in general, without pampering. Used creatively, they can make our gardens uncommonly beautiful, and they mix well with annuals, flowering bulbs, and evergreen or deciduous shrubs. Some perennials, once established, are virtually indestructible. Herbaceous peonies,

Perennials are excellent companions for other types of plants, including grasses and shrubs as well as other flowers.

for example, will bloom year after year for a century. My neighbor has varieties he dug from his grandmother's garden, and I'm certain that his grandchildren will be digging from his.

This is a book about survivors. Rather than listing every perennial known to North America, I've compiled a connoisseur's choice. Here you'll find a careful selection of those perennials that will produce the biggest impact in your garden, from flowering favorites like irises and poppies to those that produce lovely foliage effects like silvery lamb's ears and lustrous hostas.

Be assured, also, that the photography in this book features gardens of exceptional merit that show realistic ideas for home gardeners, rather than difficult-to-emulate exotic perennial gardens. I prefer to look for inspiration to perennial gardens at places like Doe Run Farm in Pennsylvania, Wave Hill in New York, Prescott Park in New Hampshire, and Western Hills in California, among others.

Finally, I want to explode a few myths. Some people have the notion that perennials are expensive, are slow to establish, and that they need good drainage. Not so. At

Cedaridge Farm we established a colorful perennial garden in just one season using inexpensive mail-order plants, and though we have a sloping site the soil has poor drainage. We not only have boggy

Left: Sneezeweed and coreopsis grow cheerfully in a sunny spot. Above: The Asiatic hybrid lily 'Enchantment', planted here with catmint, is one of the most popular garden lilies.

soil along a stream that threads through the property, we have places where water stands permanently year-round. Yet these wetland areas are alive with color all through summer because we have chosen the right plants.

Silvery-leaved artemisia, salvia, and *Canna* 'Elma Cole' create a subtle design that capitilizes on foliage interest.

Another myth is that for colorful floral arrangements you need a cutting garden of annuals. At Cedaridge Farm our most spectacular floral arrangements are all made from perennials. Visit any florist and you will see that some of the most widely used (and expensive) cut flowers are delphiniums, lilies, peonies, asters, and hostas, perennials all. One of the most enjoyable summer projects my wife and I engaged in was the production of a book entitled *Flower Arranging with Perennials*, which we wrote for Spring Hill Nurseries.

Perhaps the happiest result of gardening with perennials is the many friends we have made through sharing our garden and our plants. We will readily part with a cutting or division of anything that takes a person's fancy, and many visitors have returned to our garden with something they thought we would like. If this book makes a few more friends, we will be very pleased.

Derek Fell
Cedaridge Farm
Gardenville, Pennsylvania

Designing

with

Perennials

Opposite: Perennial sunflowers and summer phlox make perfect partners in a midsummer display.

Above: This stunning mix of daylilies, phlox, and evening primroses combines large- and small-flowered species in a range of delicate shades for added visual interest. Right: A profusion of brightly colored perennials embellishes the fronts of charming old houses.

It's not enough to simply put a collection of perennial plants into the ground; you'll want to plan for pleasing visual effects. Consider a tapestry garden, which takes full advantage of leaf shapes, textures, and colors. Or think about creating sculptural compositions that use shape and form as part of the picture, or color harmonies that establish a particular color theme or combine colors in interesting ways.

It is also essential to group together plants with similar needs. Sun-loving, drought-tolerant plants like coneflowers and daylilies thrive in open, meadowlike sites; bog-loving plants like the giant reed are best planted at moist streamsides; and shade-tolerant plants like ferns and hostas flourish in woodland gardens. Though many woodland plants, like foamflowers and cardinal flowers, may do well in full sun, they can look totally out of place in grass gardens and may even perish for lack of adequate moisture.

The best perennial garden designs help to link the landscape to the house. For example, rather than placing a kidney-shaped bed alone in the middle of a lawn, consider connecting it to a corner of the house so that it either becomes an extension of the structure or acts as a transition between the house and the natural landscape.

Color Harmonies

I am particularly fond of plantings that take into consideration an attractive background. Plantings that echo or contrast with the color of a barn, a house, a dark hemlock hedge, a stretch of glittering blue water, or a bright green sunlit meadow enhance both the character of the setting and the individual flowers.

Above: Tickseed, lilies, phlox, and peonies in soft pinks and in yellows from pastel to bold present a pleasing wash of color. Left: A cottage at Cedaridge Farm is dressed by showy, large-flowered, purple clematis.

Color harmonies help make perennial gardens special. For inspiration, look to the color combinations found in nature: birds, butterflies, seashells, and sunsets are all examples of nature's stunning palette. The hues used in the fabrics and pottery of primitive cultures are another valuable source of ideas for color combinations, as are the works of painters such as van Gogh and Matisse.

Looking at the Garden

At intervals during the growing season I often go into my garden with a box of watercolor paints and render the landscape not as it looks but as I *want* it to look, dabbing a splash of blue here, a sweep of yellow there. Then I visit local nurseries to buy plants so that I may "paint" the landscape the way I have visualized it on paper.

I also like to use the viewfinder of my camera to help create pleasing compositions, and often set my camera on a tripod to study a particular flower bed and decide if the composition can be im-

The top ten most popular perennials are all dramatic flowering plants that make a strong color impact in the landscape:

- daylilies • hostas • astilbes
- bearded irises (shown here)
- peonies • garden lilies
- oriental poppies • black-eyed Susans • phlox • Michaelmas daisies (also known as New England asters)

and phlox are my favorites), but also boast decorative silvery leaves. I think that other strictly monochromatic schemes tend to look boring, but bold swaths of a single color heightened by an accent color (such as red with silver or blue with white) can be truly stunning. Avoid strong clumps of white, however, since they tend to punch "holes" in the landscape. White in combination with

Left: Standing back and viewing your garden objectively—as if it were a framed picture—will help you identify areas where you'd like to plant more flowers or perhaps change a color. Below: A one-color scheme incorporates yarrow, lilies, bee balm, and penstemon in shades of deep red; tinges of white and light cinnamon in the yarrow add spirit to the design.

proved. If there are distracting gaps in my planting—perhaps bare soil or a patch of green where a flowering plant would make the design more interesting—then I will readily fill in the spaces. Through the viewfinder I can also better judge whether a plant is out of place and in need of moving.

One-Color Schemes

All-white is extremely popular as a color theme, especially for gardens that are meant to be enjoyed at night or frequently serve as a venue for weddings. Many perennial plants not only have beautiful white blooms (foxgloves, lilies,

other colors is most effective when used as "glitter"—rather than concentrating the white blooms in clusters, sprinkle them liberally throughout the garden. Those plants with airy flower sprays, like dame's rocket, baby's breath, foamflower, and *Gaura lindeimeri* are particularly suitable for a glitter effect.

The Impressionist's Approach

Showy blanket flowers, daylilies, and black-eyed Susans in the glorious tints of a tropical sunset make a hot color combination worthy of any Impressionist painter.

Many of the best color harmonies are created by borrowing the hues found in Impressionist paintings, notably the gardens and landscapes painted by Monet, Renoir, and van Gogh. Blue and yellow, orange and violet, and red and green—all opposites on the color wheel—are color contrasts that were admired by the Impressionists and that make fabulous flower combinations. Also consider the impact of "cool" color harmonies (blue, pink, and mauve, for example) and "hot" color harmonies (such as yellow, orange, and red). Cool colors grouped together look sensational in morning light, while hot colors become almost fiery in the warm light of a setting sun.

Certain flowering shrubs make good companions for perennials. My personal favorites include rhododendrons, forsythia, deutzia, rose of Sharon, spiraea, smoke bush, blue mist shrub, camellias, roses, dwarf lilacs, and Chinese redbud. Also consider planting compact shrubs with ornamental leaves, like purple-leaf barberry, dwarf blue spruce, and burning bush (its scarlet autumn foliage is especially beautiful when planted behind amber-colored fountain grasses). Shown here are 'Elizabeth' rhododendrons and yellow candelabra primroses.

For long perennial borders it's a lovely idea to plant flowers in colors that follow the color wheel. Begin with any color on the wheel and plant blooms in each succeeding color, repeating the first color you used at the end of the border. This repetition holds the design together, framing the entire composition. For example, flowers of creamy white merging into yellow, followed by blue merging into purple, then pink and red merging into orange, and finally a repetition of cream and yellow create just one spectacular look that you can devise using this simple plan. Repetition of shape and texture is an important element in many perennial garden designs.

Polychromatic combinations are among the most difficult to achieve because a lot of distinct colors grouped together may simply compete for attention. This effect can be garish if a

Above: Irises and poppies in violet and orange illustrate the impact of combining opposites on the color wheel, while peonies contribute splashes of white. Below: Blues, mauves, and shades of pinks—mostly from asters—make up a cool color palette in this lightly shaded spot.

mixture of disparate, brightly colored flowers is thrown together without some careful thought. One way to reconcile several different vibrant colors is to use flowers that all come from the same plant family. Rainbow mixtures of daylilies, bearded irises, or yarrow are excellent candidates. I am extremely fond of mixing bearded irises into a single bed; bicolored varieties that have a splash of white produce a gorgeous shimmering effect. Viewed through half-closed eyes or a telephoto lens, the iris flowers seem to flicker like light brushstrokes on an Impressionist painter's canvas.

Tapestry Effects

Take advantage of leaf colors to create a tapestry effect, a soothing visual delight that can capitalize on plants in a single family (like hostas and grasses) or may combine many foliage colors in a pleasing tableau that recalls a weave of fabric. Tapestry gardens not only showcase the many gradations of green, blue, yellow, and bronze that are evident in the leaves of perennial plants, but also highlight their richly textured surfaces and their fascinating leaf shapes (from slender, arching grasslike leaves to the massive heart-shaped leaves of hostas and butterbur). Bronze is a particularly important foliage color for its strength

Flowering perennials mixed with ornamental grasses, shrubs, and small trees create a natural-looking landscape that takes advantage of leaf color and texture as well as bloom color.

Perennials with Outstanding Foliage Interest

With the exception of the ferns, the following varieties also create a good flowering display. Asterisked varieties are evergreen.

Achillea species (yarrows)—gray-green fern leaf foliage.

* *Acorus gramineus variegatus* (sweet flag)—sword-shaped, white striped foliage.

Aegopodium podagraria variegatum (bishop's weed)—green and white ivylike leaves.

* *Ajuga reptans* (common bugleweed)—lustrous bronze and pink forms.

Alchemilla mollis (lady's mantle)—blue-green ivy-shaped leaves.

Artemisia species (wormwoods)—fine silver foliage.

Arundo donax variegata (giant reed)—cornlike silver and green foliage.

Athyrium niponicum pictum (Japanese painted fern)—silvery foliage.

Begonia grandis (hardy begonia)—translucent begonia leaves.

* *Bergenia cordifolia* (heartleaf)—ruffled, glossy, leathery leaves.

* *Cerastium tomentosum* (snow-in-summer)—silvery indented foliage.

Chrysanthemum pacificum (Pacific chrysanthemum)—variegated pachysandralike foliage.

* *Dianthus gratianopolitanus* (cheddar pink)—silvery grasslike foliage.

Dicentra eximia (fern-leaf bleeding heart)—feathery leaves.

* *Doronicum cordatum* (leopard's bane)—ivy-shaped leaves.

Epimedium species (bishop's hats)—heart-shaped leaves.

Geranium species (cranesbills)—indented leaves.

* *Helleborus orientalis* (Lenten rose)—leathery, evergreen leaves resembling pachysandra.

Hosta species (plantain lilies)—large, textured, paddle-shaped leaves.

* *Iberis sempervirens* (candytuft)—low, mounded habit.

* *Lamium maculatum* (dead nettle)—silvery mintlike foliage.

Ligularia dentata (ragwort)—large, bronze leaves.

* *Liriope muscari* (mondo grass)—clumping, grasslike foliage.

Matteuccia struthiopteris (ostrich fern)—fern fronds resembling a shuttlecock.

Petisites japonicus (butterbur)—gigantic heart-shaped leaves.

Polygonatum falcatum variegatum (Solomon's seal)—arching wands of white striped leaves for shady places.

* *Pulmonaria saccharata* (lungwort)—straplike marbled leaves.

* *Santolina chamaeciparissus* (lavender cotton)—fine, silver foliage.

* *Sempervivum* species (hen and chickens)—succulent bronze, blue, green, or silver rosettes.

* *Stachys olympica* (lamb's ears)—silver, velvety leaves.

* *Thymus serphyllum* (creeping thyme)—mat-forming foliage strong enough to walk on.

* *Vinca minor* 'Green and Gold' (periwinkle)—smooth, rounded green and white ground-hugging leaves.

* *Yucca filamentosa* (Adam's needle, needle palm)—spiky green or variegated leaves.

in association with green. My favorite bronze-foliaged plants include dahlia 'Bishop of Llandaff' which carries the bonus of crimson flowers and *Ligularia dentata* 'Othello', which bears yellow, daisylike flowers.

At Cedaridge Farm the most beautiful tapestry effects are along a leafy tunnel. The arching branches of native sugar maples and ashes meet overhead to form a cathedral of dappled shade, while the understory is planted with a wonderful carpet of decorative foliage plants that include shade-tolerant ferns, mosses, grasses, and hostas.

Right: This arbor entrance welcomes visitors to a path edged with blue lavender and foliage of varying colors, ranging from deep green through yellow to silver. Below: Grasses add flair to a cottage and blend beautifully with a vast array of perennials, including red montbretia.

The Joys of Ornamental Grasses

Though ferns and hostas are well known and respected for their beautiful, long-lasting foliage, especially in shady areas, ornamental grasses are only just beginning to be fully appreciated for their ability to stand alone in an ornamental grass garden. At Cedaridge Farm we have several areas devoted almost entirely to ornamental grasses.

I first became fascinated with ornamental grasses as a result of the photog-

raphy of Eliot Porter, whose careful photographic compositions of sedge grasses and desert grasses suggest a tranquility and remoteness that is soothing to the senses. When a publisher invited me to photograph 250 varieties of ornamental grasses for a book on the subject, I tackled the assignment with the challenge of evoking Eliot Porter's sensitive images.

Above: Amber feather reed grass is a good textural accent in company with red bee balm and pink summer phlox. **Below:** Ornamental grasses come in a range of colors, from palest beige to deep green, and in a variety of forms, including tufted, mounding, arching, and upright.

When planting an ornamental grass garden it's a good idea to start with 5-foot (1.5m) maiden grasses *(Miscanthus)*, as they tend to be the dominant plants. Maiden grasses are not as tall as some of the giant reeds, but they're bulky, with masses of slender, arching leaves that rustle in the slightest breeze and silky flower plumes that can be silver, red, or white. After planting the maiden grasses, I then place the fountain grasses, such as *Pennisetum alopecuroides*, mixing the varieties with pink flowers and those with black flowers. The foun-

tain grasses turn a lovely beige color in autumn, but at 3 feet (90cm) tall don't attain the height of the maiden grasses. Next come the blue fescues, which form bristly low cushions that look like sea urchins from a distance.

Carex is a large family of grasses that tolerates both boggy and dry soils. The gold form, 'Bowles Golden', is the finest of all grasses for light shade, even more desirable than the queen of clump-forming grasses, Japanese hakone grass. Though slow-growing, Japanese hakone grass looks exquisite cascading its green or variegated gold leaves along a shady path. In sun, the leaves of the variegated

Right: This grass mixture includes fountain grass (foreground). Below: This striped giant reed looks spectacular among papyrus and sedges.

form turn pink in autumn. These grasses are so beautiful that they will even hold their own as container plants.

Japanese blood grass is aptly named, since in September it turns a vibrant red, livening up the landscape like no other grass. But even the most skillful mixing of ornamental grasses can seem boring without some flowering plants interspersed. I strongly recommend lavender, especially the hardy 'Munstead Blue.' Clumps of hardy hibiscus also make appropriate highlights, with dinner plate–sized flowers in white, pink, and crimson among the greenery.

Pink coneflowers and yellow black-eyed Susans are sensational planted among grasses, since they look so natural (indeed, they do grow wild out on the prairie). Wispy blue Russian sage (*Petrovskia*) and 'Autumn Joy' sedum are also perfectly at home among grasses.

Joe Pye weed *(Eupatorium maculatum)*

Butterbur *(Petasites japonicus)*

Perennials for Structural Accents

Alcea rosea (hollyhock)—tall, spirelike beauties with an extensive color range.

Arundo donax (giant reed)—sturdy reed that grows up to 18 feet (5.4m) tall.

Erianthus ravennae (ravenna grass)—arching foliage and tall, silvery flower plumes that grow up to 12 feet (3.6m) tall.

Eupatorium maculatum (Joe Pye weed)—smoky pink flower plumes that grow up to 6 feet (1.8m) tall.

Heracleum mantegazzianum (Chinese rhubarb)—rhubarblike leaves and 10-foot (3m)-tall flower stalks.

Onopordum acanthium (Scotch thistle)—thistles with branching stems and silver foliage; grows to 8 feet (2.4m) tall.

Petasites japonicus (butterbur)—huge, heart-shaped leaves that reach up to 3 feet (90cm) across.

Rudbeckia nitida 'Herbstonne' (autumn coneflower)—branching stems 8 feet (2.4m) tall topped by yellow flowers.

Verbascum densiflorum (candelabra verbascum)—yellow flower spikes up to 6 feet (1.8m) tall and silvery foliage.

Structural Accents

Many perennials have unremarkable flowers but contribute wonderful shapes from a special arrangement of stems and leaves. The most important to consider are those with spirelike or tall, branching stems that extend interest high into the sky. I particularly like the tall candelabra shape of silvery Scotch thistles and the rocketlike flower spikes of common mullein, which make dramatic sculptural accents.

Top: The elegant spires of black hollyhocks tower over drifts of white phlox. To the left, purple loosestrife lends its spiky presence. Above: 'Stella d'Oro', one of the most admired of the daylily cultivars, is underplanted with silver-leaved artemisia for a lovely lawn border.

Beds and Borders

The difference between a bed and a border is significant, for each requires a different planting discipline; both, however, are ideal places to display perennials. A bed is generally an island of soil surrounded by lawn or paving, while a border is usually backed by a structural feature, such as a hedge, wall, or fence.

Beds and borders can be either formal or informal in design. Formal beds are usually square, rectangular, or round, while informal beds may be kidney-shaped or serpentine. Tall plants in formal island beds are best positioned in the middle, but in informal beds they can be scattered to form peaks and valleys. Similarly, in formal beds low-growing

These sample garden designs provide glorious color through three seasons of the year. While you wait for perennial plantings to mature, fill in any gaps with annuals or biennials.

Island Bed

This design features a birdbath, bench, and lace-leaf Japanese maple for added interest.

Plant List (both plans)

A Hollyhocks	I Asiatic lilies	P 'Johnson's Blue' geraniums	W Dianthus
B Delphiniums	J Daylilies		X Lupines
C Summer phlox	K Peonies	Q 'Autumn Joy' stonecrop	Y Pink evening primroses
D Miscanthus	L Russian sage	R Yarrow	Z 'Moonbeam' coreopsis
E Yuccas	M Bee balm	S Creeping phlox	AA Clematis vines (for arbor)
F New England asters	N Shasta daisies	T Red-hot pokers	
G Bearded irises	O 'Goldsturm' black-eyed Susans	U Coneflowers	BB Blue fescue
H Oriental poppies		V Ajuga	CC 'Goblin' gaillardia

Border Planting

Two dwarf Alberta spruce, an evergreen hedge (such as white pine), a stepping-stone path, an arbor with seat, and a flagstone path (or grass as an alternative) are added attractions in this design. A clematis vine, for training up the arbor, is also included.

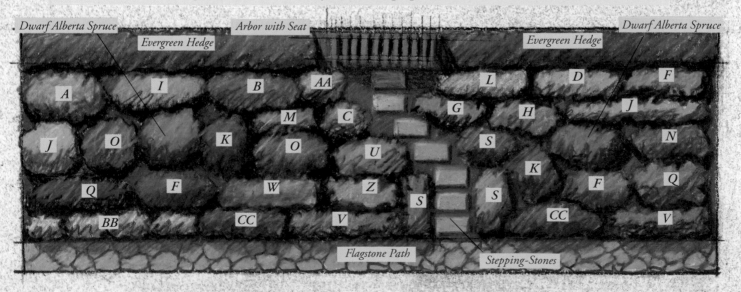

What a difference a few months can make! The outlines of these irregular island beds (below) are clearly visible in early spring before plants begin to bloom. By the middle of summer, the sweeping beds (right) are a perfect foil for the rustic charm of the springhouse here at Cedaridge Farm.

parallel beds end with a decorative feature, such as a garden statue, an archway, or a gazebo.

Free-form borders—such as serpentine ones—are highly effective at the edges of a lawn. They make excellent transition areas between lawn and woodland or lawn and meadow. Serpentine borders also help to break the monotony of house foundations, softening the straight lines of brick and clapboard.

It is important for beds and borders to have fertile, crumbly soil, dug to a depth of 2 feet (60cm). Raising the beds facilitates good drainage, another critical factor in growing beautiful, healthy perennials. (See Site Preparation [page 51] for the correct procedure.) Also, always scale beds and borders to a size that complements their surroundings. A bed that is too small or narrow will be dwarfed by the rest of the landscape, lessening the impact of the planting and wasting your hard work.

Evergreen hedges—particularly evergreen hemlock, evergreen yew, and the faster-growing evergreen arborvitae—make excellent backgrounds for perennial borders. Since it takes time for young hedge plants to fill in and reach a respectable height, you may want to use a temporary background such as a stockade or basket-weave fence. In windy situations, choose wind-resistant hedge plants like Russian olive or privet.

plants are best positioned around the edge, but in informal beds they can be alternated with medium-height plants to create a ribbon of low hills.

In formal borders tall plants work best at the back, with short ones positioned close to the front, but in informal borders tall plants like red-hot poker can be brought forward to create sculptural accents and exclamation points. Informal borders benefit from an edging of both low, carpeting plants like creeping Jenny and mound-shaped plants like 'Johnson's Blue' geranium. An occasional tall plant among them can create an explosion of flowers and leaves.

The double border is a classic perennial design. These parallel beds dissected by a path are best planted so that something is always coming into bloom. Parallel borders work particularly well when the same plants or colors are echoed on opposite sides and when the

Flowers are repeated on both sides of this double border, giving the design a pleasing sense of harmony.

Biennials can be extremely important supportive players in perennial borders. In their first year these plants germinate and produce seedlings; in their second they flower and then die. Biennials are great for temporarily filling in spaces while you wait for other plants to mature. Plants such as Scotch thistle, Canterbury bells, clary sage, sweet William, foxgloves, money plant, and verbascum must be started from seed in late summer in order to flower the following season. First start the seeds in a seed flat and then transfer the resulting seedlings to pots for sizing-up. Allow them to overwinter in a cold frame or hoop house and plant them in the garden the following spring.

Sub-shrubs are a type of perennial that bridges the gap between herbaceous perennials, which have soft stems, and woody plants, like trees and shrubs. Though soft-stemmed when juvenile, sub-shrubs develop woody stems with age. They are often classified as shrubs in catalogs and botanical reference books, but they are perfectly at home in the perennial garden. English lavender and tree peonies are both excellent sub-shrubs for perennial beds and borders.

Rock Gardens

The delicate flowers of false indigo grow happily in this rocky field as tendrils of honeysuckle clamber over a boulder; feel free to mix perennials with vines, evergreens, biennials, and other plants to arrive at a design that suits your needs.

To be successful, a rock garden should be planted on a gentle slope, allowing the rocky ledges to form naturalistic terraces for spreading plants to cascade over. A slope also provides for the construction of a stream, which will add lovely splashing sounds and tiny pools in crevices. If the rock garden is sited in full sun, then grow a rich assortment of cheerful alpine plants; if the garden is shady, foliage plants such as ferns, mosses, and hostas may need to predominate.

Rock gardens do not need to be expansive to impress. At Cedaridge Farm we built a small, sunny rock garden around two pre-fab pool liners, positioned so one would spill water into the other by means of a recirculating pump. The pools contain miniature water lilies and the edges are landscaped with ornamental grasses interplanted with alpines such as blue Dalmatian bellflowers, yellow alyssum, pink creeping phlox, yellow *Sedum acre*, and fragrant cottage pinks.

Dalmatian bellflower *(Campanula portenschlagiana)*

Perennials for Rock Gardens

These plants are all well suited for rocky landscapes.

Ajuga reptans (common bugleweed)—blue.

Armeria maritima (thrift)—pink.

Aurinia saxatilis (basket of gold)—yellow.

Campanula portenschlagiana (Dalmatian bellflower)—blue.

Cerastium tomentosum (snow-in-summer)—white.

Dianthus plumarius (cottage pink)—pink.

Erigeron species (fleabanes)—lavender-blue and pink with yellow centers.

Euphorbia polychroma (cushion spurge)—yellow.

Helianthemum nummularium (rock rose)—red, orange, yellow.

Iberis sempervirens (candytuft)—white.

Lavendula angustifolia (English lavender)—blue.

Opuntia humifusa (hardy prickly pear)—yellow.

Polygonum bistorta (knotweed)—pink.

Saponaria ocymoides (soapweed)—pink.

Sedum species and hybrids (stonecrops)—yellow, red, pink, white.

Yucca filamentosa (Adam's needle, needle palm)—white, some varieties with golden foliage.

Rock gardens have been described by some as the most amount of work for the least amount of satisfaction. But how untrue! Indeed, rock gardens can provide endless enjoyment in an extremely small space with very little care. A rock garden at Cedaridge Farm that is 10 by 10 feet (3 by 3m) has been designed around two small pools (constructed using rigid liners), one spilling water into the other. The edges of the pool are decorated with stones arranged to form ledges, and the slopes of the garden are planted primarily with ornamental grasses, including the drought-tolerant fountain grasses, maiden grass, fescues, carex, and sea oats. This rocky retreat requires little maintenance, and the music of splashing water makes it a favorite place to relax and contemplate the garden.

Water Gardens

A planting of Siberian irises, which tolerate moist or dry soil, gives character and color to this peaceful streamside.

Water gardens can take many forms, and at Cedaridge Farm we have them all, including a waterlily pond edged with plantings both in and out of the water; a stream with lush plantings and a Japanese-style arched bridge from which we can view the moon's reflection; a series of waterfalls in both sun and shade; and a swampy area with bog-loving plants like candelabra primulas and pitcher plants. Best of all, these several water gardens all interconnect: water from the pond cascades over a stone spillway to start the stream garden; waterfalls along the stream fill the air with their musical splashing sounds; and low spots along the stream create a permanently moist soil for several bog gardens. In places the water is still and deep, creating exquisite reflections; elsewhere it is shallow and glittering. Even the waterfalls employ different designs: the spillway creates a solid sheet of water; a series of broken falls funnels the water to the left and right; and an arrangement of gradual rock ledges creates the sensation of rapids.

There is an amazing diversity of plants that grow happily beside water: floating plants like water lilies will decorate the surface of the water itself; marginal plants (such as flag iris and cattails) will grow with their roots permanently immersed in water, cre-

Mixed varieties of plantain lilies (*Hosta*)

Variegated sweet flag (*Acorus calamus* 'Variegatus')

Perennials for Water Gardens

Following is a list of plants specially suited to boggy soils and wetlands. Asterisked varieties will grow with roots covered with shallow water.

* *Acorus calamus* (sweet flag)—variegated leaf blades.

Alchemilla vulgaris (lady's mantle)—lime-yellow flowers, velvety leaves.

Arum italicum (Italian arum)—lime flowers, red berries.

Astilbe × arendsi (false goatsbeard)—red, pink, white.

* *Caltha palustris* (marsh marigold)—yellow.

Helenium autumnale (sneezeweed)—yellow, orange, red, plus bicolors.

Hibiscus moscheutos (hardy hibiscus)—red, pink, white, most with contrasting eyes.

Hosta species and hybrids (plantain lilies)—white, lavender, blue, some fragrant.

* *Iris ensata* (Japanese iris)—blue, purple, white.

* *Iris pseudacorus* (flag iris)—yellow.

Iris sibirica (Siberian iris)—blue, white.

Ligularia dentata (ragwort)—yellow.

Lobelia cardinalis (cardinal flower)—crimson and pink.

Lobelia syphiltica (blue lobelia)—blue.

* *Lotus nelumbo* (sacred lotus)—pink, white.

Lysymachia punctata (yellow loosestrife)—yellow.

Lythrum salicaria (purple loosestrife)—mostly shades of pink and purple.

* *Myosotis scoparius* (forget-me-not)—blue, pink, white.

* *Nymphaea* species and hybrids (waterlilies)—white, pink, red, yellow, orange.

Primula japonica (candelabra primrose)—white, pink, red.

Typhia species (cattails)—brown.

Trollius europa (globeflower)—yellow.

* *Zantedeschia aethiopica* (calla lily)—white.

ating a transition between the water and the land; bog-loving plants like marsh marigolds and cardinal flowers grow well in swampy soil; and some edging plants, such as astilbes, ferns, and hostas, do better in high ground and thrive in cool, moist, but well-drained soil.

Right: At a pond's edge in my garden at Cedaridge Farm, garden loosestrife, clustered bellflower, and salvia admirably fill a boggy spot. Below: Creeping phlox in shades of pale pink and blue along with delicate white foamflowers brighten this woodland garden.

Shade Gardens

Given the choice I would much rather live in a sunny location than a shady one, and the flowering plant kingdom seems to feel the same way, since there is a much wider choice of ornamental plants for sun than for shade. Moreover, the deeper the shade, the more difficult it is to find suitable hardy perennial flowering plants.

The difficulty of gardening in shade is not just a question of poor light, but often it is also a matter of poor soil—especially under trees where tree roots can sit close to the ground and steal the available nutrients. Often, simply creating a raised bed with a circle of stones or thick sections of tree branches can allow good topsoil to be hauled in and a suitable planting surface to be established. However, try to keep the topsoil away from the trunk, since soil piled high around a trunk may cause rot. If this is unavoidable, never cover more than 10 inches (25cm) of the existing exposed section of trunk.

The problem of poor light is often a question of degree and of establishing the right kind of shade for plants recommended as shade-tolerant. Tests in light laboratories have shown that 1 percent more light can create a 100 percent improvement in flowering. Therefore, if you have a heavily shaded area where little will grow, removing even a single overhead tree limb or increasing nearby reflective surfaces (such as walls and fences) by painting them white can significantly improve the chances of flowering.

Purple and yellow candelabra primulas, blue forget-me-nots, and lush blue-leaf hostas thrive in this moist, shady, woodland garden.

Since many shady areas are caused by trees, an informal woodland-style garden is a natural solution for shady situations. Even a small grove of trees can be threaded with

Foxglove (*Digitalis grandiflora*)

Flowering Perennials for Shade Gardens

Note that the emphasis here is on flowering kinds. Mosses, ferns, and shrubby groundcovers with inconspicuous flowers (such as wintergreen and bearberry) are excluded.

Aquilegia species (columbines)—mostly yellow, blue, and pink.

Anemone nemerosa (wood anemone)—white.

Astilbe × arendsi (false goatsbeard)—pink, purple, red, white.

Brunnera macrophylla (perennial forget-me-not)—mostly blue.

Cimicifuga racemosa (snakeroot)—white.

Chrysogonum virginianum (gold stars)—yellow.

Dicentra species (bleeding hearts)—mostly pink and white.

Digitalis species (foxgloves)—purple, white, yellow.

Doronicum cordatum (leopard's bane)—yellow.

Epimedium species (barrenworts)—pink, yellow, and white.

Geranium maculatum (cranesbill)—pink.

Helleborus orientalis (Lenten rose)—mostly white, pink, and maroon.

Hosta species and hybrids (plantain lilies)—white, blue, lavender.

Lobelia cardinalis (cardinal flower)—crimson.

Liriope species (mondo grass, lily turf)—purple.

Mertensia virginica (Virginia bluebells)—blue.

Phlox divaricata (wild blue phlox)—blue.

Polemonium caerulea (Jacob's ladder)—blue.

Poligonatum biflorum (Solomon's seal)—white.

Primula species (primrose)—yellow, orange, white, red, blue, maroon.

Pulmonaria saccharata (Bethlehem sage)—pink, blue, white.

Sanguinaria canadensis (bloodroot)—white.

Tiarella cordifolia (foamflower)—pink, white.

Uvularia grandiflora (merrybells)—yellow.

Vinca minor (periwinkle)—blue.

Viola species and hybrids (violets)—white, yellow, blue, red.

a charming wood-chip path with accompanying plantings of both flowering and foliage perennials. Contrasting leaf colors (such as silvery Japanese painted ferns and dark green violas), textures (such as velvety leaves of honesty and lustrous *helleborus* foliage), and shapes (such as feathery maidenhair ferns and heart-shaped hostas) supply additional interest to the woodland garden. Tucked among the tapestry of foliage, colonies of shade-loving flowering perennials—notably lemony English primroses, blue forget-me-nots, and pink bleeding hearts—bring a dash of color.

Also, consider some tender perennial bulbs, like caladiums and tuberous begonias. If brighter floral color is desired, plant some colonies of perennial blue phlox *(Phlox stolonifera)*, perennial violas like Johnny jump-ups, and even add a splash of electric color here and there with shade-tolerant annuals such as impatiens, wishbone flower, and coleus.

Nor should you overlook the value of some shade-tolerant ornamental grasses, which are perfect for edging woodland paths. Two excellent candidates are *Carex*

Pink and white Lenten roses nod gracefully at the base of a tree. These early-blooming beauties are favorites for woodland walks and forest edges.

elata 'Bowles Golden' and Japanese hakone grass *(Hachonecloa macra)*, either the dark green or the golden form, 'Aureola', which changes to a pinkish red in autumn. The leaves of these clump-forming grasses spread out like a fan and look sensational spilling into a path.

Every shade garden has a transitional area (such as the edge of a wood or the east or west side of a building), which receives both sun and shade as the sun crosses the sky. Some excellent transitional plants include foxgloves, foamflowers, wild blue phlox, and goatsbeard.

To carry color higher into the tree canopy, some shade-tolerant flowering shrubs, such as azaleas, rhododendrons, and hydrangeas, can be added in the background.

Formal shade gardens work well in courtyards and city plots where tall buildings or boundary walls throw shade over the garden. Geometrically shaped shade gardens are traditionally edged with dwarf boxwood, and many low, bushy perennial plants serve the same purpose but have the added bonus of flowering. These include mondo grass, dwarf hostas, primulas, violas, and even alpine strawberries (also known as fraises des bois).

Above: Primroses in the popular 'Barn-haven' strain show off their spectacular, yellow-centered, pink blooms at the edge of a wide lawn. Right: Oriental poppies breathe a hint of the exotic into this formal garden.

Meadow Gardens

If anything in gardening can be called distinctly "American," it is the concept of a wild meadow garden—not the European concept of a meadow garden with annual poppies and wild oat grasses mixed among apple or olive trees, but a prairie-style garden where a rich assortment of perennial wildflowers and ornamental grasses combine to make a symphony of color in the shimmering heat of a summer's day.

All across North America—from the Great Lakes in the north to the Texas-Mexico border in the south—there are beautiful natural stretches of grassland that harbor myr-

**Evening primroses *(Oenothera speciosa)*
and Texas bluebonnets *(Lupinus texensis)***

**'Gloriosa' black-eyed Susans
(Rudbeckia hirta 'Gloriosa')**

Perennials for Meadow Gardens

The following includes flowering plants only.

Achillea species (yarrows)—white, yellow, pink, red.

Anthemis tinctoria (golden marguerite)—yellow.

Asclepias tuberosa (butterfly weed)—orange.

Aster novae-anglae (New England aster)—red, pink, blue, white.

Baptisia australis (false indigo)—blue.

Chrysanthemum leucanthemum (ox-eye daisy)—white with yellow centers.

Coreopsis lanceolata (lance-leaf coreopsis)—yellow.

Echinacea purpurea (purple coneflower)—purple, pink, white.

Eupatorium coelestinum (hardy ageratum)—shades of blue, plus white.

Eupatorium fistulosa (Joe Pye weed)—pink.

Gaillardia species (blanket flowers)—yellow, red.

Helenium autumnale (sneezeweed)—yellow, red, orange, plus bicolors.

Helianthus species (perennial sunflowers)—yellow.

Heliopsis helianthoides (false sunflower)—yellow.

Hemerocallis species (daylilies)—yellow, orange.

Liatris spicata (bottlebursh)—purple.

Lobelia cardinalis (cardinal flower)—red.

Lupinus species (lupines)—blue, white, pink.

Monarda didyma (bee balm)—red, pink, white, burgundy.

Oenothera species (evening primroses)—pink, yellow.

Papaver orientale (Oriental poppy)—red, pink, white, plus bicolors.

Phlox subulata (summer phlox)—red, pink, white.

Physostegia virginiana (obedient plant)—pink.

Rudbeckia hirta (black-eyed Susan)—yellow.

Rudbeckia triloba (autumn coneflower)—yellow.

Vernonia noveboracensis (ironweed)—purple.

iad first-rate perennials, including black-eyed Susans, purple coneflowers, blanket flowers, and bottlebrush. In addition, these prairies are home to a splendid assortment of graceful grasses, such as switch grass, bluestem, and Indian rice grass. This combination of grasses and wildflowers can produce spectacular effects on a large or small scale. At Cedaridge Farm we have several large-scale meadow gardens of more than 5 acres (2ha) each, plus a small meadow garden that serves as a transition between the cultivated areas of the garden and the natural meadowland.

Small- and large-scale meadow gardens demand quite different planting methods. Small meadow gardens may be more intensively planted. Start by tilling a serpentine bed for perennial plants to be set out in small colonies. These include purple coneflowers, yellow black-eyed Susans, some species lilies such as *Lilium candense* and *L. specio-*

sum, plus dame's rocket, butterfly weed, species daylilies such as *Hemerocallis citrinus* and *H. fulva*, and ox-eye daisies. You may want to separate the colonies with plantings of local switch grass *(Panicum virgatum)*, fountain grass *(Pennisetum alopecuroides)*, and maiden grasses (*Miscanthus sinsensis* varieties).

For larger meadow plantings, make free-form island beds and direct-seed the site with a colony of wildflowers. Good choices for direct-seeding are indigenous kinds like pink milkweed, purple ironweed, magenta Joe Pye weed, yellow black-eyed Susans, purple coneflowers, pink dame's rocket, purple foxglove, white or pink penstemon, and yellow hawkweed. Some introduced meadow wildflowers like hybrid blue or pink lupines, yellow yarrow, and white ox-eye daisies are also successful when they are direct-seeded.

In both large and small meadow gardens, it's desirable to include some flowering annuals—such as scarlet corn poppies, blue cornflowers, pink cosmos, and bluebonnets—for dramatic effect.

Meadow gardens are best when they have a natural, unplanned look. Yellow plains coreopsis and white Shasta daisies convey a sense of the wilderness in this exuberant meadow planting.

Growing Perennials

Opposite: Summer-flowering perennials and ornamental grasses are natural companions.

Most hardy perennials are tenacious, requiring little more than adequate soil depth to accommodate their often vigorous root systems and a light high-phosphorus fertilizer (such as bone meal) in order to produce their best flower displays. Other maintenance chores are elementary: watering during dry spells (a good soaking around the

roots whenever a week goes by without a good penetrating rain); staking of tall growing varieties (like delphiniums and peonies); hoeing or mulching to keep down weeds; and some winter preparation to protect against prolonged freezing weather.

Right: Mulching will help keep your perennial garden free of weeds. Below: Feathery, white false goatsbeard and the 'Morden's Pink' variety of purple loosetrife are happiest in moist soils—once planted, they are trouble-free.

Variety Selection

Variety selection is extremely important not only when you want a garden that is special in terms of hardiness and color, but also to ensure superlative long-lasting floral displays. Some varieties are simply superior to their brethren, and it's to your advantage to grow these varieties. For instance, a German nurseryman developed a sterile variety of the popular perennial *Rudbeckia hirta*. This variety, called 'Goldsturm', cannot produce viable seed and therefore puts all its energy into growing an unusually large quantity of flowers. 'Goldsturm' can be propagated only from cuttings, though seed-grown plants are sometimes offered by nurserymen seeking to cash in on the name; these are not the true originator's stock and produce inferior results.

The wild pampas grass *Cortaderia sellouana* is a popular summer-flowering perennial for southern gardens and other places with mild winters, such as coastal California, but it rarely survives north of Washington, D.C. The variety 'Icalma', however, was discovered growing at a height of more than 10,000 feet (3,048m) in the Andes Mountains, and has survived outdoors north of New York City. Another example of hardiness that is often overlooked is in autumn-blooming chrysanthemums. The ready-to-bloom

kinds purchased at nurseries rarely survive severe winters, but the more robust varieties 'Fantasia' and 'Prophet' will come back to grow bigger and better each successive season.

Likewise, native bleeding heart *Dicentra eximia* is a spring-flowering perennial that produces a flush of color for three weeks in early spring, but the hybrid 'Luxuriant' not only comes on strong in spring, it continues blooming until autumn frosts. Another superior hybrid perennial is *Sedum* × 'Autumn Joy'. A deeper pink than its popular parent, *S. spectabile*, it is also longer-lasting, for it changes to a cinnamon color as it ages, and when the flower heads dry they remain decorative until freezing weather.

Above: 'Autumn Joy' maintains its color over a longer period than other sedums. Below: 'Prophet' cushion chrysanthemums are extra hardy and will survive severe winters.

Reading gardening magazines, visiting good perennial plant displays at botanical gardens, and talking with experienced perennial growers are all good ways to learn about new varieties. Buying plants from reputable sources is also vital to ensure that you receive a healthy, high-quality plant.

'Tricolor' stonecrops wait in pots to be transplanted into the garden. Make sure to buy your seeds, bareroot stock, or plants only from reputable dealers for the best results.

When you buy perennials from a nursery you'll usually find plants grown in both quart and gallon containers. It's fine to buy the smaller, less expensive quart size, since perennials are quick to grow once they're transplanted. However, it is important to check the drainage holes at the bottom of the pot to see if the roots have reached the bottom. It's a good sign if they have, since perennials with weak root systems can suffer transplant shock. If necessary, knock the root ball out of the pot to see if there really is a healthy root system. By the time summer clearance sales for perennials hit, many of the plants appear tall and spindly. Cut these tall stems to within 4 inches (10cm) of the pot to stimulate new, bushy growth.

Where to Buy Perennials

The growing of perennials has become a cottage industry across North America, and it's not difficult to find local growers who offer a wide selection of ready-to-bloom varieties in sizeable pots (such as 1-gallon [3.7L] and even 3-gallon [11.3L] capacities). It is also possible in most areas to find specialty growers who deal in a particular plant family, such as peonies, daylilies, or bearded irises. These are the sources to patronize when you want to quickly establish a notable collection of a particular plant group.

For the biggest selections of perennials—especially the latest and best hybrids—mail-order sources are your best

I've made something of a hobby of collecting scarce perennials. If you see a perennial you like in someone else's garden, don't be bashful about asking for a cutting, seeds, or a division. Most gardeners are only too happy to share their treasures. My own garden is filled with plants I have traded for: a unique black columbine called 'Magpie'; an old-fashioned bronze-leaf dahlia called 'Bishop of Llandaff'; 'Gold Lace', a maroon Barnhaven primrose with yellow petal tips; and the most desirable of all the tree peonies, 'Joseph Rock', which bears huge, single, white blooms with maroon, poppylike petal markings.

bet. Some mail-order houses feature several thousand varieties, and though most offer small plants (in many cases bareroot stock that needs potting-up as soon as it is received), these plants are capable of growing quickly if they have healthy root systems and are shipped properly.

Site Preparation

The great British plantswoman Gertrude Jekyll advocated digging perennial beds and borders to a depth of 3 feet (90cm) and mixing in cartloads of well-decomposed animal manure prior to planting. If you have access to a backhoe and have the time to prepare a bed 3 feet deep, then do so, but I have found that in moderately well-drained soil a depth of 2 feet (60cm) is sufficient, especially if you can raise the soil surface about 6 inches (15cm) above the surrounding soil by edging the bed with stones, bricks, or landscape ties and filling with topsoil.

Good drainage is vital for many desirable perennials, particularly English lavender, bear's breeches, foxtail lilies, eidelweiss, and cottage pinks. To provide the drainage these plants need, mix plenty of fine gravel into the soil. You might also consider constructing a raised bed using flagstones around the edge, since the extra height allows water to drain freely.

Most perennial plants thrive in a neutral or slightly acidic soil. To test soil pH (its degree of alkalinity or acidity), you can buy an inexpensive meter at a garden center. This meter will give you a quick reading, and all you have to do is simply push the probe into the soil. If the reading indicates that your soil is heavily alkaline, you should add sulphur. Too acidic a soil requires the addition of lime. However, I recommend that you purchase a kit that can be mailed to a soil test laboratory. These tests, which can be purchased from large garden centers or at your county agent's office, provide pH readings that are much more accurate, and the printout you receive will tell you exactly how to correct any pH imbalance. As an added bonus, with a professionally tested soil sample you'll also learn of any nutrient deficiencies and will receive advice on how to correct them.

Double digging is the best way to prepare your soil for planting and I especially recommend it if you're digging to a depth of only 2 feet (60cm). This technique involves removing any sod from the top of the soil, digging to a depth of 12 inches (30cm)—the length of a spade—and placing this layer of topsoil to one side (on a tarp). Next, dig down another spade's depth and place this second layer of soil (the sub-

soil) on another tarp. Then take a garden fork and fork over the bottom, mixing in a 4-inch (10cm) layer of humus, such as garden compost, peat, or well-decomposed animal manure. Spade the topsoil layer back into the hole where the subsoil layer used to be, again mixing in at least 4 inches of humus. Finally, spade in the subsoil so it now becomes the topsoil; to this layer add a 4-inch layer of humus and also a granular all-purpose plant

Above: Remove the sod, using a wooden plank laid along the border of the plot to create a nice, clean edge. Left: Next, dig to a depth of 12 inches (30cm), placing the soil to the side. As you dig, remove any rocks, wood, or other debris, since this soil will eventually be added back to the garden plot.

food high in phosphorus (such as 5-10-5). If the humus you use is in the form of garden compost or animal manure, you can skip the addition of fertilizer, since compost and manure contain all the nutrients that perennial plants will need. In the case of peat (a sterile soil conditioner), a granular fertilizer is usually necessary. If the soil needs lime (for modifying acidity) or sulphur (for modifying alkalinity), then also mix this into the final layer at the same time.

The spading and addition of humus will fluff up the soil and should automatically raise the bed about 6 inches (15cm) above the original soil level. The site is then ready to receive plants. After planting, a decorative organic mulch (such as shredded pine bark or wood chips) can be added to help control weeds and keep moisture in the soil.

Staking

It is quite disconcerting to see healthy clumps of perennials grow top-heavy and fall over, creating an untidy appearance and suffocating neighboring plants. Some (like Joe Pye weed) have such heavy flower heads that after a shower of rain they can snap off at the base of their stems or topple over completely, tearing a huge root ball out of the soil.

The most economical supports to use are bamboo poles, which can be purchased in varying lengths and thicknesses. Use them to support a single flower stem (like a trumpet lily), or make a cat's cradle with string crisscrossed over a plant to support a whole clump of stems (like hollyhocks and delphiniums).

Easier to use are plastic-coated metal supports with legs that can stand alone

Top: When you spade the layers of soil back into the plot, make sure to add plenty of humus in the form of compost, peat, or well-decomposed animal manure. Above: These peonies have been staked early with a metal plant hoop; once tall, bushy plants spread, it can be difficult to gather stalks together for staking.

or link together. I also like supports with a wide metal mesh and splayed legs for supporting bushy plants like peonies. It is important that these self-supporting devices be set in place early, before the plant has produced excessive growth, since once a plant has become leggy it is difficult to control.

Inconspicuous green twist ties are useful for tieing plant stems to bamboo poles—they're much easier to use than string, since a simple twist replaces the tedious task of knotting and cutting.

Improper staking can ruin the appearance of a perennial border. Don't be afraid to use substantial wooden stakes for the long, heavy stems of lilies, foxgloves, perennial sunflowers, and delphiniums. At Cedaridge Farm we find that bamboo canes are often inadequate, and prefer instead surveyor's stakes, which we purchase by the bundle from a local lumber company. These stakes are strong and attractive, performing the job admirably.

Left: Both Siberian irises and Oriental poppies, in this cottage garden at Cedaridge Farm, benefit from fertilizing.

Fertilizing

Some perennials, like yarrow, are perfectly content in poor soil and tend to produce too much leafy growth when fertilized heavily. On the other hand, delphiniums, bearded irises, and peonies are greedy feeders. If you have access to a lot of garden compost or well-decomposed animal manure, then a side dressing (2 to 3 inches [5 to 7.5cm]) lightly worked into the upper soil surface in spring and autumn will be sufficient to keep perennials healthy. If you are unable to maintain this regimen, a light application of a granular (or liquid) fertilizer should be worked into the soil either in autumn after frost or in spring before new growth is far advanced.

Winter Protection

Perennials vary widely in their degree of hardiness. Tender perennial bulbs like calla lilies and caladiums will not tolerate frozen soil and should be lifted each year for storage in a frost-free room. Borderline hardy perennials (such as pampas plume and Peruvian lilies) can be planted in sheltered locations and mulched with shredded leaves or similar organic material to help them through the winter.

Temperature is not the only factor governing the hardiness of plants. Exposure to wind, poor drainage, and a variety unsuitable for the particular situation are all factors that can kill perennials during winter.

Winter cleanup is also important. I like to clear beds of old mulch after frost and apply new mulch, since this helps to rid the area of insects and their larvae, which can overwinter in old mulch. Also, when applying new mulch, it's a good idea to mix in some rodent repellent, since mulch attracts mice and voles, which can devastate a perennial border by feeding on the roots and crowns of plants.

Right: Hoop houses, when covered with heavy plastic, help shield plants from harsh winter winds and freezing temperatures. Below: This 3-year-old iris, shown with rhizomes exposed, is being dug so that it can be divided.

Propagation

There are basically three ways to multiply perennials—by division, from various types of cuttings (including stem cuttings, root cuttings, and leaf cuttings), and from seeds. In the A-to-Z section, Perennials of Distinction, (see page 62) I explain the best method for propagating each type of perennial plant.

Division

By far the easiest way to get more perennials is by division. Almost all perennial plants are easily divided because they create vigorous, spreading root systems. To divide, you simply dig up a clump (3-year-old clumps are best), wash away all the soil from around the roots, and separate the root mass into smaller clumps, using a trowel or a spade where the clumps are tenacious.

When you divide a clump you will usually end up with some large divisions and a lot of smaller ones. The large divisions can be planted directly into other parts of the garden, but the smaller divisions are best potted individually or held for a season in a special nursery bed to "size up," then transplanted in a "ready-to-bloom" stage. In northern gardens the greatest survival rate from smaller divisions is assured if the potted plants are held over in a hoop house or a cold frame. Hoop houses are simply metal arches covered with plastic to form a tunnel that shelters the small plants from severe weather. These hoop houses do not need to be heated, but must be strong enough to withstand the weight of ice and snow.

These small divisions will be given time to size up in pots before they are planted in the garden.

If you intend to propagate lots of perennials, a hoop house is a good investment. A hoop house is simply a metal frame covered with clear or opaque white plastic. It need not be heated and requires no foundation, but should have a floor of gravel to make a level base that can accommodate pots. The plastic will not exclude frost, but it will protect potted young divisions and rooted cuttings from severe freezing weather and wind damage, ensuring a high survival rate and strong growth for early flowering.

Cuttings

Of the three types of cuttings used to multiply perennials, the most common is a stem cutting. Simply take a 3- to 4-inch (7.5 to 10cm) section of stem with a healthy crown of leaves and strip the leaves from the bottom half of the cutting. Then dip the cut end in rooting hormone and place it up to half its length in potting soil. Plastic or wooden seed flats make it easy to accommodate a large number of cuttings at one time.

Keep the flats in a lightly shaded location, and water or mist regularly to prevent the potting soil from drying out. When a healthy set of roots has formed (usually within three months), transfer the cuttings to individual pots or directly into the garden. You'll have a higher rate of success if you loosely cover the flats with clear plastic to create a humid microclimate.

For some perennials you can take root cuttings; this method is particularly good for Oriental poppies and phlox. Simply dig up a well-established plant, wash away the soil, and cut the fleshy roots into 1-inch (2.5cm) segments. Each segment contains a growing point that will sprout roots and leaves soon after the root is covered with soil and watered. Like stem cuttings, root cuttings are best planted into flats so that a worthwhile number can be propagated at one time. You won't need to add rooting hormone to ensure success.

A few fleshy-leafed perennials, such as the hardy prickly pear cactus and some types of stonecrop, can be propagated by leaf cuttings. Simply break off a leaf from its stem, dip the broken end in rooting hormone, and place the leaf upright in potting soil to one-third its length. Again, use a flat to propagate a substantial quantity. Keep the cuttings in a lightly shaded location, since direct sunlight can harm the plants.

This seaside planting includes succulent ice plants and ivy-leaf geraniums easily propagated from stem cuttings. The ice plants also propagate from leaf cuttings.

Seeds

Many perennials are easy to grow from seeds; others are challenging; and some cannot be grown from seeds at all. It all depends on the variety. Seed starting differs from other forms of propagation discussed here in that results may vary. Though some perennials will grow "true to type" and produce an identical match with the parent, others produce variations.

Some perennials, like hellebores, will germinate quickly if the seed is fresh; others may need a chilling period in order to germinate. The best place to find all this information is on the seed packet or in the catalog description if you are purchasing from a mail-order source.

There are several methods of seed starting, depending on the variety you are growing. A few can be direct-seeded—that is, the seeds can be scattered onto the bare soil and covered lightly in the bed where you want the plants to bloom. Be sure that the soil is suited to the perennial (see Perennials of Distinction [page 62], or check the seed packet of the variety you are planting). Many wildflowers indigenous to woodlands (like trilliums and wild blue phlox) prefer a highly acidic soil, while those indigenous to prairie and desert areas (like Texas bluebonnets) prefer an alkaline soil.

Most perennials are best started in seed flats. The resulting seedlings should be transferred to individual pots once they are large enough to handle. Oriental poppies

Seedlings started in seed flats and pots are ready to be transplanted into the garden. If seedlings have been kept indoors, assure that they will survive relocation by hardening them off in a cold frame.

and primroses, for example, have high germination when the tiny seeds are surface sown onto potting soil in a seed tray and the resulting seedlings teased out for transferring to pots to size up before transplanting. Mist the flats regularly to keep soil moist and cover the flats loosely with clear plastic to create a humid microclimate.

Tiny seeds generally need light to germinate and should be lightly pressed into the soil surface. Many large-seeded perennials, like lupines, have tough, bullet-hard seed coats and require soaking overnight in water to hasten germination. Always keep seedlings out of direct sunlight and never allow the soil to dry out completely. After transferring seedlings to individual pots, fertilize them lightly to keep the plants growing strongly. If you move the plants from a warm indoor environment, like a sunroom or greenhouse, be sure to harden them off by placing them in a cold frame for a week so that they will not suffer transplant shock.

Be aware that some perennials will flower the same season after starting from seed, but others can take several years to bloom. See Perennials of Distinction (page 62) for details on flowering for specific plants.

The dwarf pampas grass 'Pumila' makes a dramatic impact planted in a container, though it needs a relatively large container like this half-barrel.

Perennials in Containers

Though most perennials can be grown in containers, many have a relatively short flowering span compared with annuals such as French marigolds and petunias. It makes sense to find subjects that either have a long flowering period—such as 'Moonbeam' coreopsis and the hybrid fern-leaf bleeding heart 'Luxuriant'—or provide a long-lasting foliage effect—such as spikey Spanish dagger and Japanese hakone grass.

Containers for perennials should provide at least 3 gallons (11.3L) of soil capacity and preferably be made of wood or clay. Whiskey half-barrels are particularly good, since they are roomy and wood provides excellent insulation

against overheating. Clay is also good in this respect, but clay pots generally need more frequent watering because of the absorption qualities of clay. Metal and plastic are poor containers for perennials,

Above left: Flax lily grows happily in a terra-cotta pot beside a pool. Above: The daylily cultivar 'Happy Returns' is another good container candidate.

since they are prone to overheating, which can cause feeder roots to become burned.

Equal parts of screened garden topsoil, peat (or garden compost), and sand (not beach sand) make an excellent soil mix for container perennials. Water the plants whenever the soil surface feels dry, and feed with a liquid fertilizer at time of watering every 2 weeks during the growing season. In addition to plants that fit comfortably in the container, consider edging the pot with perennials that will cascade down the sides (such as periwinkle) or plant a vine that can be grown up a trellis (such as clematis).

For container groupings, don't be afraid to display a variety of pots for added interest. Use a wooden half-barrel or a metal cauldron as a centerpiece, and surround it with terra-cotta pots in different shapes and sizes. If you mix and match containers, it's best to stick to simple color combinations like blue and yellow, red and pink, blue and white, or even black and white (you can find black violas, black hollyhocks, black columbines, black fountain grass, and black carnations, for example).

Perennials for Containers

Asterisked varieties are tender perennial bulbs that need to be taken inside during winter.

Begonia grandis (hardy begonia)—Features decorative leaves and nonstop bloom; plants grow 2 feet (60cm) high.

* *Begonia tuberosa* (tuberous begonia)—These everblooming plants grow 1 to 2 feet (30 to 60cm) high in a rich color range (red, orange, yellow, white, and pink).

* *Caladium hortorum* (rainbow plant)—The multicolored, heart-shaped leaves last all season.

Chrysanthemum × moriflorum—(cushion mum) Provides long-lasting autumn color; mound plants grow just 1½ feet (45cm) high.

* *Colocassia esculenta* (elephant's ears)—Offers huge, heart-shaped leaves.

Coreopsis grandiflora 'Early Sunrise' ('Early Sunrise' tickseed)—Everblooming, yellow, daisylike flowers bloom on 1½-foot (45cm)-high plants.

* *Dahlia × hybrida* (tuberous dahlia)—Many dwarf everblooming kinds are excellent for containers; the vast color range includes yellow, orange, pink, and red.

Dicentra hybrid 'Luxuriant' (bleeding heart)—Nonstop pink flowers last all season long; grows 1½ feet (45cm) high.

Hemerocallis hybrids (dwarf daylilies)—The everblooming varieties 'Stella d'Oro' and 'Happy Returns' (orange and yellow, respectively) are particularly good; these plants grow just 2 feet (60cm) high.

Lavandula angustifolia (English lavender)—Offers silvery foliage and fragrant purple or blue flowers; grows 2 feet (60cm) high.

Lilium hybrids (garden lilies)—Try 'Black Beauty' (a red Turk's cap lily), 'Enchantment' (Asiatic hybrid), and some of the Oriental hybrids such as 'Star Gazer'.

Pennisetum alopecuroides (fountain grass)—This is one of the best of the clump-forming ornamental grasses; consider also blue fescue, carex 'Bowles Golden', and Japanese hakone grass.

Rudbeckia hirta burpeeii (gloriosa daisy)—Dwarf kinds such as 'Marmalade' bloom all season.

Salvia × superba 'Lubeca' (blue sage)—Provides 14 weeks of blue flowers just 1½ feet (45cm) high.

Sedum seiboldii (seibold stonecrop)—Trailing blue-green stems and lovely pink flowers are suitable for edging containers.

Viola cornuta (viola)—Many varieties, especially the blue and yellow cultivars, will flower continuously all summer.

* *Zantadeschia aethiopica* (calla lily)—Features arrow-shaped leaves and white, hooded flowers.

'Autumn Joy' stonecrop (*Sedum* 'Autumn Joy')

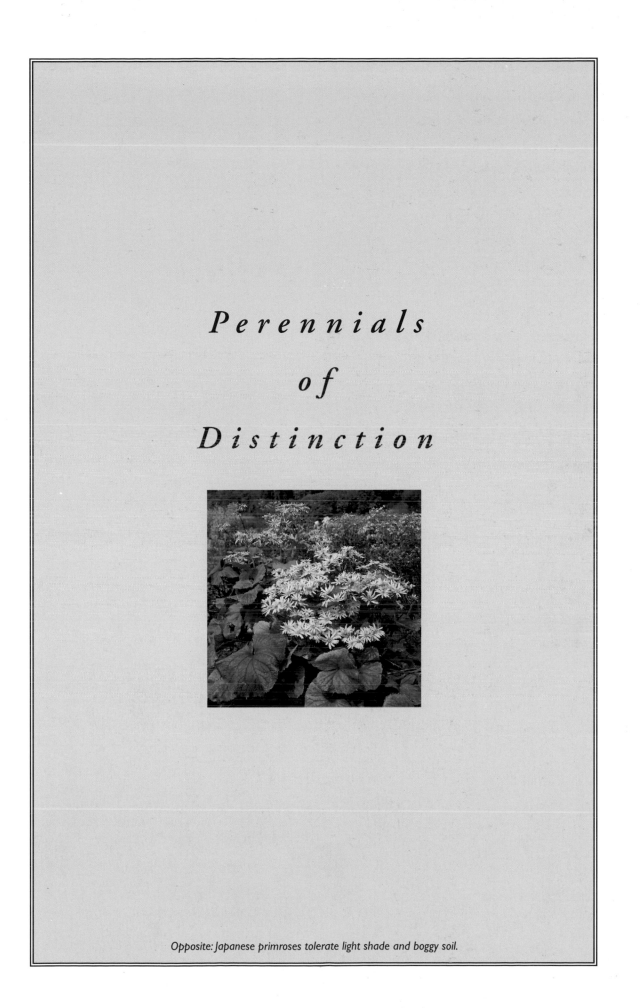

Perennials
of
Distinction

Opposite: Japanese primroses tolerate light shade and boggy soil.

The following selection of perennials is not a comprehensive list of perennial plants, but rather an elite list of those I have found most satisfying to grow. These are the plants that have produced the biggest impact in my own garden, either with their generous amounts of color, their interesting leaf shapes, or their overall structural impact on the designed landscape. Where there is a large number of varieties in a particular family (like salvias and hostas), I have tried to bring forward the "best of the bunch" and explain my reasons for choosing that particular variety.

Right: 'Summer Pastels' yarrow. Below: 'The Beacon' yarrow dominates a bed of mixed perennials.

Achillea
(y a r r o w)

The introduction of hybrids among diverse species of yarrow (mostly native to Europe and Asia) has not only produced a rainbow mixture of colors, but has resulted in cultivars such as 'Summer Pastels', which will bloom the first year from seeds. Flowers are white, cream, yellow, red, and pink. You can also propagate by division after the plant has flowered.

The flower heads of the yarrow varieties described here are all characterized by flat heads formed of clusters of tightly packed florets. Drought-tolerant and suitable for cutting, yarrow is not particular about soil as long as it drains well, but it must be sited in full sun.

Among the many yellow-flowered forms, 'Coronation Gold' is one of the best. Peak bloom lasts up to 7 weeks. A hybrid, it grows 3 feet (90cm) high, and a bonus is its silvery-gray, feathery leaves. It is wonderful in company with blue delphiniums and blue *Salvia nemerosa*.

Achillea millefolium 'Fire King', a rosy red cultivar, has proven to be longer-blooming than other yarrows. If spent flowers are deadheaded, then plants can bloom nonstop for 14 weeks, beginning in early summer.

Above: 'Coronation Gold' yarrow in mid-summer. Below: The unusual long flower spikes of 'Botanical Wonder' common bugleweed.

Ajuga reptans
(common bugleweed)

Tremendous improvements have been made to this early-flowering, mat-forming, evergreen perennial in recent years. Valued for its tightly packed, blue flower spikes, the cultivar 'Botanical Wonder' has the stateliest flowers. There are also pink and white forms that look sensational when mixed.

Also consider special selections with decorative foliage, such as 'Crisp Red'. Though the flowers are more subtle than those of other cultivars, the beautiful reddish bronze foliage stays decorative year-round and makes a sensational groundcover.

Common bugleweed grows in sun or light shade and tolerates poor soil provided that drainage is good. Propagate by division after flowering. Yellow alyssum and pink creeping phlox are good companions for bugleweed.

Anemone × hybrida
(Japanese anemone)

Valuable perennials for the late-blooming border, Japanese anemone flowers during late summer and early autumn. The variety 'Whirlwind' bears spectacular, large, semidouble white flowers that look more like clematis than anemones. Other hybrids, such as 'September Charm', are a rich, pink color. All have powdery yellow stamens at the center of the flowers, which are borne on long stems excellent for cutting.

Since plants grow to 5 feet (1.5m) tall, they generally need staking. Give Japanese anemone a fertile humus-rich soil, good drainage, and full sun, though it will tolerate light shade. The leaves are dark green and toothed, resembling ivy. Propagate by division after flowering.

Japanese anemone makes a strong accent in beds and borders, or it can be massed it at the edge of a woodland. It is an excellent companion to late-flowering asters such as 'Harrington's Pink' and sedums such as 'Autumn Joy', as well as to ornamental grasses.

Aquilegia species *and* hybrids

(columbines)

Many fine species of columbine native to North America have been crossed with European kinds to create spectacular hybrids. These are undoubtedly among the highlights of a spring garden, and can be planted in sun or light shade. The flowers are exquisite. Shaped like an old-fashioned granny's bonnet, they have the added appeal of rakish long spurs.

Indigenous to the eastern United States, *A. canadensis* is a beautiful red that produces masses of flowers on 2-foot (60cm) plants. Its yellow cultivar, 'Corbett', looks sensational massed along a woodland path or planted in drifts in a rock garden.

The hybrids tend to be short-lived as perennials, but they have the largest flowers. 'McKana Giant', for example, offers white, yellow, red, and blue with the bonus of flowers the first season if seeds are started indoors 8 weeks before outdoor planting. Given full sun and a fertile, humus-rich soil with good drainage, 'McKana Giant' will bloom for 6 weeks.

The species columbines are easily divided, though most will self-sow readily to create generous colonies. The hybrids are best propagated from seed, though seeds saved from the second generation are usually sterile or of poor quality. Columbines are good companions for woodland phlox, honesty, dame's rocket, and lupines. A combination of pink and blue columbines massed in a border or rock garden is enchanting. They are excellent for cutting.

The red pendantlike blooms of wild columbine are superb when massed.

Aster species *and* hybrids

(asters, Michaelmas daisies)

The New England aster 'Harrington's Pink' blooms for more than a month in autumn and has long stems that are good for cutting.

I t's a curious fact that many indigenous plants are rarely appreciated by gardeners in their own land. Such is the case with Michaelmas daisies—varieties of American asters that bloom in late summer and early autumn. Visit any European botanical garden at that time of year and you will see American asters and their hybrids planted prolifically in great sweeps of color. Most are derived from crosses using two main North American species—*Aster nova-anglae* (the New England aster) and *Aster nova-belgi* (the New York aster).

The New England aster is generally seen in the wild in shades of violet-purple, but there are several fine late-summer garden varieties in other colors—notably 'Harrington's Pink', which is characterized by dense clumps of soft pink flowers with bright yellow "eyes." Since the plants can grow to 4 feet (1.2m) tall, they are best planted against fences for support or staked to hold their stems erect. New England aster is a fine companion for silvery lamb's ears, variegated *Miscanthus* grass, and *Sedum* 'Autumn Joy'.

There are two exceptional blue aster hybrids, 'Monch' and 'Wonder of Staffa'. Though they look like American asters and appear to be an identical sky blue with a yellow center, they were hybridized from two Asian species. Both flower prolifically from mid-summer for up to 14 weeks. They grow to 3 feet (90cm) tall and make wonderful companions for black-eyed Susans.

Often confused with chrysanthemums (to which they are closely related), most varieties of New England and New York asters grow tall and may need staking. Unfortunately, there are few dwarf varieties, with the exception of *A. dumosus* 'Professor Kippenburg', a medium blue aster that grows to just 12 inches (30cm) tall.

Asters relish full sun and tolerate poor soil providing it drains well. Propagate by division after flowering.

False goatsbeard, a summer-bloomer, looks wonderful massed along the edges of streams and ponds.

Astilbe × arendsi
(false goatsbeard)

Remarkable, spirelike flower plumes appear in summer, notably in white, pink, and red. Peak flowering lasts about 4 weeks, but the dried flower heads remain decorative right through winter. Even when false goatsbeard is not in bloom, the small, spear-shaped, serrated leaflets are quite decorative. The best varieties are hybrids developed by a German nurseryman, George Arends—notably 'Fanal' (a deep crimson-red) and 'Rheinland' (a deep rose-pink). They make superb cut flowers. Plants grow 2 to 3 feet (60 to 90cm) high, depending on the variety.

False goatsbeard grows in sun or light shade, and thrives in both well-drained and boggy soil, especially if the soil is fertile and high in humus content. It is excellent for massing along the margins of ponds and streams. Though flowering times vary according to variety, false goatsbeard makes a good companion for yellow lady's mantle, blue Japanese iris, and yellow *Ligularia dentata*.

Left: 'Fanal' is the best red astilbe cultivar. Below: False indigo, which has long spires that resemble lupines, is a sensational plant for rock gardens.

Baptisia australis

(false indigo)

Native to Texas (*australis* is Latin for "southern") and related to lupines, these hardy plants form a dense bush of cloverlike leaves and spires of dark blue flowers, up to 4 feet (1.2m) tall. Hardy throughout North America, plants are virtually indestructible once established, since they develop a strong tap root and tolerate even impoverished soil.

Plants grow best in full sun and in soil that drains well. Flowering in spring, false indigo makes a good accent in mixed borders and rock gardens. Propagate by seeds and root division.

Bergenia cordifolia

(heartleaf)

This decorative underplanting of pink heartleaf sets off a hedge of red camellias.

Native to Siberia, these reliably hardy plants form lustrous rosettes of shiny green or bronze leaves that turn russet in autumn. The rich leaf texture is reason enough to grow this beautiful perennial, but in early spring clusters of pink, rosy red, or white flowers are borne high on slender stems that grow up to 18 inches (45cm) tall.

In light shade and a humus-rich, cool soil (such as is found in woodland and along streambanks and ponds), the plants can form dense colonies and create an attractive evergreen groundcover. They are excellent companions to ferns, hellebores, and forget-me-nots. Propagate heartleaf by root division.

Campanula glomerata
(clustered bellflower)

Of all the many hardy bellflowers, this is the showiest. Plants form bushy clumps of erect stems topped with tight clusters of bell-shaped blue blossoms that appear in early summer.

Plants prefer full sun and a fertile, humus-rich soil, and will tolerate a moist soil. They make dramatic accents in mixed beds and borders, are suitable for cutting, and combine well with yellow loosestrife, maiden grasses, and pink evening primroses. Propagate by division.

Above: A grouping of clustered bellflowers adorns a mixed perennial border. Below: Serbian bellflowers decorate the margin of a pool.

Campanula poscharskyana
(Serbian bellflower)

This low, spreading, hardy plant is perhaps the most free-flowering of all the bellflowers. Spring-flowering, it produces broad, pointed leaves that are almost hidden by masses of cheerful, sky blue flowers.

Plants prefer full sun and a loam soil with good drainage. They look especially beautiful planted at the edges of pools, with the flowers spilling into the water. They will also thrive in the crevices of dry rock walls and in rock gardens. Growing just 6 inches (15cm) tall on the flat, the vining stems will actually climb several feet up a wall. Serbian bellflower combines well with lady's mantle. Propagate by root division.

Centaurea montana

(mountain bluet)

These hardy, bushy plants have slender, dark green leaves and grow to 2 feet (60cm) tall, producing lovely deep blue flowers that resemble a giant cornflower. Blooming in late spring and early summer, mountain bluets are good companions to yellow Siberian wallflowers and late pink tulips.

Plant mountain bluets in full sun and provide good drainage. Use them as accents in beds and borders or for cutting. Propagate by division.

Above: The blue flowers of mountain bluet combine well with yellow Siberian wallflowers and red tulips. Below: A healthy planting of red valerian.

Centranthus ruber

(red valerian)

Though this hardy, bushy plant is tolerant of dry conditions, it performs best in coastal locations and during cool weather. Red, rose-pink, or white cone-shaped flower clusters generally appear in late spring. The slender, spear-shaped green leaves and the red or rosy forms are particularly appealing, especially when planted close to delphiniums, shrub roses, and the geranium hybrid 'Johnson's Blue'.

Plants prefer full sun and excellent drainage, grow to 3 feet (90cm) tall, and may require staking. Because of their long stems, they make excellent cutting flowers, and they look good in rock gardens and planted as colonies on slopes. Propagate by seeds or root division.

Chrysanthemum
species *and*
hybrids

The 'Prophet' series of cushion chrysanthemums are extra hardy and usually come back to flower year afer year.

Alarge family of sun-loving, daisy-like perennials that resemble asters, chrysanthemums generally bloom earlier in the season. Several varieties are outstanding—*C. coccineum* (commonly called painted daisy or pyrethrum) is notable for its beautiful spring blooms in red, pink, and white, all with yellow button centers. Growing 3 feet (90cm) tall, with strong stems suitable for cutting, painted daisies are exquisite in combination with peonies, bearded irises, Oriental poppies, and lupines. They flower for up to 6 weeks.

Chrysanthemum frutescens (Marguerite daisy) is a little too tender to overwinter outdoors in northern gardens, but it is good for growing in containers. Plants produce so many flowers that they almost completely cover the serrated foliage. Bloom colors include white, pink, and yellow in singles and doubles. Marguerite daisies are especially popular in California gardens, where they will create magnificent mounds of flowers in flushes throughout the year if deadheaded. Plants demand full sun and good drainage, and grow to 5 feet (1.5m) tall. They can be easily trained to a single stem to make a "tree daisy" up to 5 feet high.

Chrysanthemum maximum (Shasta daisy) is sometimes listed as *C. superbum.* 'Alaska' is the most popular variety, for its large, white daisylike heads that reach up to 4 inches (10cm) across with bright yellow button centers. These summer-flowering plants grow to 2½ feet (75cm) tall, and have long, strong stems excellent for cutting. There are several excellent dwarf forms that produce compact cushions. The best of these is 'Snow Lady' (15 inches [38cm] tall), which blooms nonstop for up to 10 weeks.

Chrysanthemum × moriflorum (cushion mum) is invaluable for its late summer and autumn color, though ready-to-bloom cushion mums bought from nurseries often do not have the hardiness to survive winter. Two outstanding groups of cultivars that are sufficiently hardy for northern gardens are the Prophet series and the Fantasia series. The color range is mostly russet colors—yellow, red, pink, orange, bronze, and purple, plus white. Instead of purchasing ready-to-bloom plants in late summer, consider buying rooted cuttings by mail for spring planting. An added bonus of mail ordering is lower cost. When planted in

A beautiful mass planting of Shasta daisies decorates a perennial garden in early summer, with yellow and blue flag irises filling in the background.

spring, these rooted cuttings need to be pinched back several times in order to make them branch. This will create a desirable compact cushion effect and an average height of 15 inches (38cm). Peak flowering occurs for up to 6 weeks in September and October. After 3 years clumps can be divided.

Chrysanthemum rubellum 'Clara Curtis' resembles the painted daisy, but its 3-inch (7.5cm), clear, pink blooms continue nonstop for up to 12 weeks beginning in early summer. It is sensational in combination with delphiniums.

Above: A clump of white Marguerite daisies form the plant's typical dome of white flowers. Right: 'Moonbeam' coreopsis blooms nonstop all summer long.

Coreopsis verticillata

(threadleaf coreopsis)

Native to North America, plants feature cushions of delicate, feathery foliage and cheerful, yellow, star-shaped flowers. The lemon-colored variety 'Moonbeam' is one of the wonders of the perennial kingdom, flowering for up to 10 weeks from early summer to autumn frost.

Threadleaf coreopsis grows just 1 foot (30cm) high, and is excellent for edging and massing in rock gardens. It prefers full sun and good drainage, and tolerates poor soil. Propagate by division after flowering. Threadleaf coreopsis makes a good companion for white Shasta daisies, red and yellow Indian blanket, and blue Stokes asters.

Corydalis flexuosa
(blue bleeding heart)

A recent introduction from China, the variety 'Blue Panda' can be a sensational component of shady places, such as a path's edge in a woodland garden or the lightly shaded bank of a pond. The hardy, mounded, spring-flowering, bushy plants grow in clumps of feathery, blue-green leaves. Masses of flower stems are crowded with blue, trumpet-shaped blooms that from a distance resemble those of the fern leaf bleeding heart.

Plant in full sun and provide good drainage. Use blue bleeding heart as an accent in mixed beds and borders or as a cutting flower. This perennial is best propagated by division.

Above: 'Blue Panda' bleeding heart thrives in light shade. Below: English delphiniums decorate a rose garden in late spring.

Delphinium elatum
(delphinium)

F or a tall, elegant, spirelike flowering accent, nothing compares with the English delphinium. Unfortunately, it is best suited to a maritime climate, like that of coastal California and coastal Maine, and its flowering display can be short-lived elsewhere. The delphinium is a popular cut flower, and it's difficult to have too many of them in the garden. Though not reliably hardy in many northern gardens, mulching can help a good percentage through the winter. Its cut-flower value alone makes it worth

building a special raised bed that can be covered with glass or plastic sheeting during winter. This shelter will provide delphiniums with the extra protection they sometimes need to get them through a severe cold spell.

The Pacific Giants series is the most reliable of the tall varieties, particularly a special selection of the blues known as 'Round Table' hybrids. They are superb when planted beside vining clematis and climbing roses. Though the predominant color is blue, colors include white, purple, and even pink. At the center of each flower is a contrasting, butterfly-shaped arrangement of inner petals known as a "bee," which can be white or black depending on the variety.

Delphiniums need a sunny site and fertile soil with plenty of humus. To maintain a cool soil temperature during summer, a covering of organic material (such as shredded leaves, straw, or wood chips) is advisable. Be sure to water frequently during dry spells. Provide strong supports for tall varieties.

Though delphiniums can be propagated from division and also from cuttings taken from new shoots, the Pacific Giants are easily raised from seed, starting in the autumn prior to their blooming season, or 12 weeks ahead of transplanting.

Dianthus plumarius

(cottage pink, grass pink)

A drift of cottage pinks in shades of red appreciates excellent drainage and thrives on sunny slopes.

There are many kinds of dianthus that are good for massing along dry slopes or for edging mixed borders. Cottage pinks are not only among the hardiest, they are the showiest, and are capable of producing so many flowers that the blooms almost hide the blue-green, grasslike leaves. Flowering in late spring, the blooms on most varieties are double, highly fragrant, and resemble miniature carnations.

Plants grow to 12 inches (30cm) tall, have a low, mounded, spreading habit, and prefer full sun in well-drained soil. Colors include pink, red, purple, and white, as well as several bicolors. Important components of rock gardens, they are usually short-lived as perennials, but are easily propagated by root division, layering, and stem cuttings.

Dicentra spectabilis
(bleeding heart)

'Luxuriant', a bleeding heart hybrid, flowers nonstop from May through October.

Native to Japan, bleeding heart blooms for 6 weeks in early spring, producing graceful, arching flower wands tipped with pendant, heart-shaped pink flowers. Graceful, 3-foot (90cm)-high, shrublike clumps of blue-green shamrocklike leaves are an added bonus and will give the plant ornamental value after blooms have faded. Though suitable for full sun, provided the soil has plenty of humus to keep it cool, bleeding hearts relish a lightly shaded location. Though the pink is beautiful, the white variety, *D. spectabilis* 'Alba', looks especially good in shady areas and all-white gardens. Plants normally go dormant by midsummer.

Bleeding hearts prefer a humus-rich, well-drained soil. They are exquisite for woodland gardens in company with purple honesty and wild blue phlox. The foliage contrasts well with ferns and hostas. Propagate by division after flowering.

Dicentra × 'Luxuriant' (fern leaf bleeding heart)—a hybrid cross between an American species and a Japanese species—is possibly the longest-flowering perennial you can have in your garden, since plants will start the season off with a flush of heart-shaped pink flowers in early spring and continue nonstop until autumn frost. Plants are much smaller than the old-fashioned bleeding heart (reaching just 15 inches [38cm] high), and the flowers are born on erect, rather than arching, stems. The white variety, 'Alba', will bloom for 12 weeks nonstop.

Plants prefer a humus-rich soil in light shade, but will tolerate full sun if the soil can be kept cool by mulching. Fern leaf bleeding heart is a good companion for bluebells, forget-me-nots, and primroses. Propagate by division.

Summer-blooming purple coneflowers and pink double-flowered hollyhocks make excellent partners in this sunny flower bed.

Echinacea purpurea
(purple coneflower)

Native to North American prairies, these daisylike plants look like pinkish purple black-eyed Susans, and bloom about the same time, in midsummer. The large flowers have swept-back petals and a conspicuous, chocolate-colored dome at the center. The cultivar 'Bright Star' has the largest flowers (up to 5 inches [12.5cm] across), while 'White Luster' is a pure white form. Both are excellent for cutting.

Plants flower for 8 weeks starting in early summer. They demand full sun and tolerate poor soil, provided drainage is good. In addition to mixed borders, coneflowers are suitable for meadow gardens. Propagate 3-year-old clumps by division. Coneflowers are good companions for ornamental grasses, black-eyed Susans, and summer phlox.

Euphorbia polychroma

(cushion spurge)

These dazzling spring-flowering plants (also known as *E. epithymoides*) form perfect mounds just 18 inches (45cm) high, covered in flat, circular yellow flower clusters that will outshine anything else in the garden in early spring. Even when cushion spurge is out of bloom, the succulent blue-green leaves remain decorative.

Plants prefer full sun, and tolerate poor soil provided it is well drained. Propagate by division after flowering and by stem cuttings. Cushion spurge is excellent for rock gardens and makes a good companion to candytuft, forget-me-nots, and late-flowering tulips.

Above: Cushion spurge typically forms dense clumps. Below: Dwarf blanket flower 'Baby Cole'.

Gaillardia × grandiflora

(blanket flower)

Native to North America, wild gaillardia species grow to 3 feet (90cm) tall, and produce yellow, daisy-like flowers with red zones at the petal centers. 'Burgundy', a tall hybrid, displays wine-red flowers, and is suitable as a border accent or for massing in a meadow garden. Its long stems make it good for cutting.

Several dwarf varieties such as 'Baby Cole' and 'Goblin' are excellent for edging beds and borders. If faded flowers are deadheaded, these cultivars will bloom nonstop for up to 14 weeks, producing beautiful cushions of bloom with bicolored yellow and red flowers that often completely hide the foliage. These dwarf kinds are excellent companions for yellow threadleaf coreopsis and blue fescue ornamental grass.

Geranium ×
'Johnson's Blue'

(blue geranium,
blue cranesbill)

The geranium 'Johnson's Blue' starts flowering in spring and will repeat its bloom if spent flower stems are cut back.

There are vast numbers of hardy geraniums offered for perennial gardens. The majority do well in a cool maritime climate like the Pacific Northwest, but they tend to be shy-flowering over the rest of North America, with the notable exception of a generous-flowering hybrid, 'Johnson's Blue'. Believed to be a cross between a European and Himalayan species, the beautiful mounded plants are covered with 2-inch (5cm)-wide flowers and attractive, serrated green leaves. Following a first flush of bloom, the plants can be cut back to force new flower buds and a second flush.

Good for sun or light shade, plants look especially attractive in combination with yellow sundrops, yellow loosestrife, and pink foxgloves. Give geraniums a fertile soil with good drainage, and divide clumps after 3 years to keep them vigorous.

Helenium autumnale

(sneezeweed)

Native to boggy stream and river banks in the eastern United States, sneezeweed grows to 6 feet (1.8m) tall, becoming top-heavy with masses of daisylike yellow or red flowers for 4 to 6 weeks in late summer. Unless they are staked, the tall kinds will invariably fall over. Use sneezeweed sparingly except in association with giant-size, late-blooming perennials such as Joe Pye weed, plume poppy, and maiden grass. There are several superb dwarf varieties that don't need staking, including 'Gypsy' and 'Wyndley', both with bronze and golden flowers on bushy plants just 3 feet (90cm) tall.

Plants are easily propagated by division. Give sneezeweed full sun and a fertile, moist soil.

Helenium 'Gypsy' is an unusual dwarf variety. Most other varieties of sneezeweed are tall and generally need staking to prevent them from toppling over.

Helianthus × multiflorus

(perennial sunflower)

These wonderful, yellow, daisylike flowers are perfect for the midsummer border, especially in combination with summer phlox. The perennial sunflower takes over when its look-alike (the false sunflower) starts to dwindle. Plants grow to 5 feet (1.5m) tall and produce masses of semidouble flowers borne on strong stems suitable for cutting. The cultivar 'Flore Pleno' has double flowers, and grows to 6 feet (1.8m) tall. 'Flore Pleno' flowers nonstop from midsummer to autumn frost, but it needs strong staking to keep it erect.

Plants prefer full sun and good drainage. Three-year clumps should be divided to keep them in bounds. Perennial sunflowers are particularly effective as a tall background for yellow black-eyed Susans.

Left: Perennial sunflowers (at the back of the border) look sensational when paired with black-eyed Susans, here seen in mid-summer. Below: 'Karat' ox-eye daisies bloom in late spring.

Heliopsis species

(ox-eye daisies, false sunflowers)

There are two North American heliopsis species—*H. scabra* and *H. helainthoides*—that provide bold yellow accents in perennial borders. With their similar, daisylike flowers, both on 4-foot (1.2m) stems, you can hardly tell the two species apart. For my money, the variety 'Karat' is superior simply for the immense size of its flowers—up to 5 inches (12.5cm) across. The false sunflower is a superb cut flower, resembling an annual sunflower.

Plants prefer full sun; they tolerate poor soil provided drainage is good, and need dividing after 3 years. The serrated, spear-shaped leaves are borne on strong stems that seldom need staking. Plants are also similar to *Helianthus × multiflorus*, but flower earlier. False sunflower makes an excellent companion for trumpet lilies, Carolina phlox, and catmint.

Helleborus orientalis

(*Lenten rose*)

Two fine colors of the Lenten rose bloom in my garden at Cedaridge Farm.

Several species of helleborus make fine, early-flowering perennials. The best known is perhaps the Christmas rose *(H. niger)*, which bears white blooms with a powdery yellow crown of stamens, but it is not nearly as hardy, nor as free-flowering, nor as colorful, nor as easy to grow as the Lenten rose *(H. orientalis)*, which also starts to bloom between Christmas and March, depending on how far south you live. The Lenten rose produces masses of nodding, cup-shaped flowers up to 2½ inches (6.3cm) across. The white, pink, or maroon flowers, some with contrasting freckles, are held in generous clusters above serrated, leathery, evergreen leaves that resemble pachysandra.

Lenten roses form clumps up to 1½ feet (45cm) tall, and are best planted on slopes, where the pendant flower clusters can be fully appreciated. Sometimes, a New Zealand variety called 'White Magic' is offered by nurseries who claim that it's a hybrid of *H. orientalis* and *H. niger*, but it is clearly *not* since *H. orientalis* and *H. niger* are incompatible as parents. Actually, 'White Magic', which boasts flowers measuring up to 4 inches (10cm) across, is raised from seed from a large-flowered selection of *H. niger*. 'White Magic' is identical to 'Potter's Wheel', a large-flowered British variety, and indeed is probably a selection out of 'Potter's Wheel'.

Lenten roses do not transplant well once established, and division is unreliable. Propagate them from seed, making sure the seed is fresh, since aged seed sometimes requires two winter periods to break dormancy. Seedlings occur readily among adult plants, and when small they may be teased from the soil and transferred to pots or nursery beds to size up.

Lenten roses prefer a fertile loam soil with plenty of humus. Light shade is best, but they will tolerate sun if they are heavily mulched with leaf mold or peat to keep the soil cool. During severe winters the leaves may turn brown, but if these brown leaves are removed at the onset of spring weather, the roots will send up new leaves along with the flower buds to create a beautiful display. Lenten roses make excellent companions for daffodils, or they can be planted under early-flowering shrubs such as yellow witch hazels, yellow forsythia, pink and red quince, white magnolias, or pink *Rhododendron mucronulatum*.

The dwarf orange daylily 'Stella d'Oro', planted with 'Silver Brocade' artemisia and pink Carolina phlox.

Hemerocallis species *and* hybrids
(daylilies)

What daffodils are to spring, daylilies are to summer. They seem to tolerate every kind of climate and planting site, with the exception of deep, dark shade and constantly boggy soil. They survive heat and drought better than any other perennial I know. With some of the dwarf varieties, such as 'Happy Returns', the floral display can last for 10 weeks or more.

Surprisingly, the wild daylily you see along the roadsides of North America is an immigrant from China. The beautiful, orange, trumpet-shaped flowers and tawny petal markings bloom for about 3 weeks, though each flower lasts only a day, opening in the morning and wilting by dusk. These wild daylilies form fountainlike clumps of sword-shaped green leaves. Planted on dry slopes, they effectively control erosion. For beds and borders, however, the hybrid daylily is king.

Modern hybrid daylilies come in a wide range of colors, including white, cream, yellow, red, pink, lavender-blue, orange, mahogany, green, and various bicolors. Some are classified as "dormants," which means they lose their leaves in winter, while others are classified as "evergreen." Generally, the dormants are hardier than the evergreens. Unless a description specifies that a daylily is "evergreen," the variety is most likely a dormant form.

The most free-flowering daylily is 'Stella d'Oro', an American hybrid that grows low and compact (just 18 inches [45cm] high). The golden yellow blooms usually begin in May and continue nonstop until October, provided the spent blooms are removed. Another good, long-flowering hybrid is the yellow-flowered 'Happy Returns'.

Fragrant daylilies are scarce: one that has gorgeous flowers as well as a pleasing scent is 'Hyperion', a large, lemon yellow cultivar. For even larger size (but no fragrance), consider 'Mary Todd', which bears golden yellow blooms. Also take a careful look at the 'Siloam' hybrids. Many of these are remarkable for their bicolored effects— 'Button Box', for instance, is a stunning yellow with a prominent burgundy eye zone; 'Ethel Smith' is apricot with pink, yellow, and green tones in the throat. Seek out a local specialist grower or mail-order source for these and other excellent varieties.

Plant miniatures 1½ feet (45cm) apart and regular varieties 2 feet (60cm) apart. Feed daylilies in early spring and again after autumn frost with a high phosphorus fertilizer for best results. Propagate by division after the third season. They are excellent companions to garden lilies, coneflowers, black-eyed Susans, Shasta daisies, yarrow, and summer phlox. Use daylilies also among ornamental grasses and on dry banks at the edges of ponds and streams.

Like 'Stella d'Oro', the dwarf yellow daylily 'Happy Returns' is suitable for containers and blooms until autumn frost.

Hibiscus moscheutos 'Southern Belle'

(common rose mallow, swamp rose mallow)

Hibiscus moscheutos 'Southern Belle' has gigantic flowers the size of dinner plates.

Though wild species of hardy hibiscus are native to North America, a Japanese breeder—Takeo Sakata—produced 'Southern Belle', a variety that flowers the first year from seed.

The seeds of 'Southern Belle' are hard, but if you soak them overnight before planting and start them indoors 8 weeks before you plan to transplant outdoors, the flowers will bloom by midsummer and continue until autumn frost. The size of dinner plates (up to 10 inches [25cm] across), 'Southern Belle' hibiscus comes in white, pink, and red. Each flower lasts a day, but there are enough buds on each flower stem to ensure nonstop blooms for 8 weeks.

Left in the ground, 'Southern Belle' will rebloom each year, making thicker clumps that can be divided. It likes full sun and tolerates moist soil, making an excellent com-

Hosta species *and* hybrids
(hostas, funkia, plantain lilies)

panion to cardinal flowers, Joe Pye weed, maiden grass, and cattails at the edges of streams and ponds.

Since plants will grow to 5 feet (1.5m) tall, staking is advisable. Also, the leaves are attractive to Japanese beetles and caterpillars, so spray them with a safe insecticidal soap solution. 'Disco Belle' is a dwarf cultivar, with slightly smaller flowers, but after the first season it matches the height of 'Southern Belle'.

The varietaged hosta 'Ellerbrook' makes a beautiful streamside planting; here it is paired with vibrant pink and yellow candelabra primulas.

Hostas have become such favorite shade plants in recent years that they rival daylilies, irises, and peonies in popularity. Native to Japan, there are hostas in sizes to suit every need—small ones (8 to 12 inches [20 to 30cm]) for edgings and rock gardens; groundcover varieties (1½ to 2 feet [45 to 60cm]) with vigorous, spreading horizontal growth; and background hostas (2 to 3 feet [60 to 90cm]) for strong accents in perennial beds and borders. Though hostas are grown mainly for their broad, paddle-shaped, decorative leaves, most have bold white or pale lilac flowers, and some are heavily fragrant. Most varieties can be planted in sun or shade; if you plant hostas in the sun, though, they need extra humus in the soil, mulching to conserve soil moisture, and watering during dry spells. They are happiest in a fertile, partly shaded, moist, humus-rich soil.

One of the most popular of all specialist perennial books is *The Hosta Book* by hybridizer Paul Aden. My favorite of all hostas—'Blue Angel'—is a Paul Aden original. An excellent background plant, it produces huge, heavily textured, blue leaves and a prodigious number of white flowers the size of foxgloves.

When I judge the quality of hostas I look first at leaf coloration and shape, but also take into account the texture of the leaf surface, which can be handsomely blistered like a savoy cabbage. Many hostas' leaves turn a beautiful golden color in autumn.

The most widely planted hosta, *H. seiboldiana* 'Frances Williams', forms 4-foot (1.2m) -wide clumps of heart-shaped leaves that are not only savoyed, but also enhanced by prominent leaf veins. The center of each leaf is a glossy blue-green, while the edges are streaked with golden yellow. Pale lilac flowers appear in early summer and are excellent for cutting. The bold summer foliage turns orange in autumn.

After leaf color I look for a free-flowering habit. 'Fragrant Bouquet' is my favorite, since its huge, white, honey-scented, funnel-form flowers are the largest to be found among the hostas, and they bloom at the same time as black-eyed Susans, which I like to use as a companion plant. In shade, 'Fragrant Bouquet' makes a perfect companion to ferns, especially the ostrich plume.

Hostas are wonderful for dressing up a bed along a shady house foundation, and are also excellent for lining shady driveways and ringing trees. Because hostas drop their leaves after frost and don't break dormancy until late spring, they are excellent companions to daffodils, covering dead bulb foliage after the display has finished. In dry, sandy soil or heavy clay soil, dig in plenty of garden compost, leaf mold, or peat to improve texture and moisture-holding capacity.

About the only pests that present a serious threat to hostas are snails and slugs, which may chew holes in the leaves. These creatures can be controlled by sprinkling slug bait among the plantings or by hand picking populations in the early morning when their silvery trails reveal their presence.

Iris ensata
(Japanese iris, sword-leaved iris)

Every water garden and streamside planting should feature a solid mass of Japanese irises. Even though they love a sunny or lightly shaded position and moist soil (they'll even grow with their roots permanently covered with shallow water), Japanese irises are also content in soil with good drainage and in partially shaded positions.

Flowering in midsummer, Japanese irises come in all shades of blue, as well as purple and white. Individual flowers

A mass planting of Japanese irises graces a streamside in my garden.

can grow to 6 inches (15cm) across, and make wonderful companions for waterlilies. Propagate by division in autumn. By planting a wide selection of Japanese, bearded, and Siberian irises, it's possible to have irises flowering from early spring until late summer.

This gorgeous border of bearded irises features a stunning mixture of colors, including coppery orange, lemon yellow, and pale blue.

Iris × germanica
(bearded iris, flag iris)

The bearded iris is a truly remarkable flower, not only for its extensive color range and easy care but also for the high esteem in which it is held by artists and gardeners. The French Impressionist painter Claude Monet collected iris varieties, and one of Vincent van Gogh's iris paintings holds the world record for the highest price bid at auction.

At Cedaridge Farm we use bearded irises in borders all to themselves and also blended with other perennials, especially dame's rocket, peonies, and Oriental poppies. An iris border of mixed colors is an uplifting sight because bearded irises offer more colors than any other family of perennial. The color range is so extensive that every color of the rainbow is present, in so many variations they almost defy classification. Some of the more unusual colors are ginger, green, and black. Some iris collections (such as the Presby Iris Gardens in Montclair, New Jersey) contain as many as three thousand varieties and cultivars.

Developed from complex crosses among European species, bearded irises are suitable for all but the most tropical parts of North America. Their swollen roots (called rhizomes) love sharp winters, and they enjoy being baked in warm, sunny summers.

Though spring is the peak flowering period for most bearded irises (generally around Memorial Day), hybridizers are now producing new strains of repeat-blooming iris, capable of flowering again in late summer or early autumn. For rebloom to occur, the plants must be watered during dry spells, and also must be given a booster side-dressing of a high-phosphorus fertilizer like bone meal between flowering.

The flower structure of a bearded iris is composed of three broad petals that sweep down (called falls) and three that arch up (called standards). The wider the falls and the more pronounced the arching, the better the iris. At the throat of each flower is a prominent arrangement of powdery stamens called a beard. A pronounced beard that complements the petal colors is considered highly desirable.

Iris flowers may be a single solid color (like 'Blue Sapphire'), or they may be bicolored (like 'Tollgate', a blue and white cultivar) or tricolored (like 'Old Master', which is a tan, yellow, and violet mix). Bicolors that feature white in the standards (like 'Gay Parasol') are particularly appealing because the white helps the iris to present a glittering effect when massed in borders.

Flowers of the bearded iris last only a day, though several flowers on a stem can be open at any one time, with more buds lower on the stem to prolong the flowering season. Deadheading of the spent flowers is advisable.

Though maintenance-free once planted, bearded irises prefer full sun and a well-drained soil. If the soil is sandy or clay, work in some humus such as well-decomposed animal manure or garden compost. If the soil drains poorly, construct a raised bed to remedy the situation. Bearded irises are greedy feeders and will thrive with applications of fertilizer in spring before blooming and again in autumn after frost. Divide clumps after the fourth season, cutting the clumps with a sharp spade into segments with two or three rhizomes (swollen, sausage-shaped organs that grow partially underground).

Iris sibirica
(Siberian iris)

Though not long-lasting in flower, Siberian irises are valuable for late-spring color along streams and ponds, where they tolerate moist or dry soil in full sun. Also use them as accents in mixed perennial borders, especially in combination with yellow loosestrife and red Oriental poppies. Growing 3 to 4 feet (90 to 120cm) tall, Siberian irises form thick clumps, which should be divided after 3 years.

In late spring, bold blue Siberian irises and European ox-eye daisies create a stunning floral display.

Liatris spicata 'Kobold' does not grow as tall and ungainly as other varieties. It tolerates the heat well, blooming in midsummer. This flower looks especially good when partnered with ornamental grasses.

Liatris spicata
(blazing star)

Native to North America's prairies, this clump-forming, erect plant produces strong, pokerlike flower stems with narrow, grasslike leaves all the way to the flower head. The flowers are usually purple, and look like a fluffy bottlebrush. Growing to 4 feet (1.2m) tall, the flowers are excellent for cutting and are also ideal for meadow gardens. Give them full sun and good drainage.

The wild species may be a bit too tall and coarse for perennial gardens, but the variety 'Kobold' is a dwarf selection that is excellent in combination with daylilies and ornamental grasses.

Lilium species *and* hybrids
(garden lilies)

Garden lilies are a diverse group characterized by beautiful trumpet- or chalice-shaped blooms. Though individual flowering time is relatively short (usually 4 weeks), if you choose your varieties carefully it's possible to have lilies in bloom from late spring into autumn. Many of the best are quite hardy and do not deserve their reputation for being difficult to grow. Indeed, many are as easy to grow as daffodils, coming back every year and multiplying freely. Lilies thrive in both full sun (provided the soil is mulched to keep it cool) and light shade. Since most garden lilies grow long stems (3 to 5 feet [90 to 150cm] long, depending on the variety), they look best when planted among lower-growing ferns and hostas in shady locations or salvias and coreopsis in sunny places.

Undoubtedly the most popular lily for perennial gardens, the midsummer orange-flowered Japanese tiger lily (*L. lancefolium*, also known as *L. tigrinum*) grows to 6 feet (1.8m) tall. Because of its spectacular height, it generally needs staking. Tiger lilies make good companions to pink summer phlox and black-eyed Susans. Also, they look sensational planted in a colony near the dark red Turk's-cap lily, 'Black Beauty'.

The most progressive bulb breeder in North America was the late Jan de Graaff, a Dutchman who immigrated to Oregon and founded a lily-breeding business near Portland. I first met de Graaff at the Mayfair Hotel in London, where he invited me to help launch his new strains of lilies into Europe. After a press luncheon for British garden writers and a successful launch, he encouraged me to move to America.

De Graaff eventually retired from his lily-breeding business, and the rights to his name have passed to Spring Hill Nurseries, which still conducts mailings offering some of de Graaff's most stunning varieties.

Perhaps de Graaff's most famous variety is 'Enchantment'. An orange-flowering Asiatic hybrid, this lily produces glorious, upward-facing, chalice-shaped blooms. A

beautiful companion to 'Enchantment' is the yellow-flowered 'Connecticut King' (not a de Graaff introduction). There is also a wonderful mixture of Asiatic hybrid lilies called the 'Mid-Century' hybrids. They look much like 'Enchantment' (in fact some nurseries call them 'Enchantment' mixed), but are available in white, pink, red, purple, yellow, and maroon in addition to orange. They are as easy to grow as daffodils. Just give them a humus-rich, fertile, well-drained soil—in either sun or light shade—and they will not only come back every year, but will multiply freely. When you buy a mixture described as "naturalizing," it is usually the 'Mid-Century' hybrids.

The Asiatic hybrid lily 'Enchantment' is as easy to grow as a daffodil.

After the Asiatic hybrids, introduce your garden to some of de Graaff's spectacular Oriental hybrids, particularly any of the 'Imperials'. 'Imperial Silver', which bears heavily spotted white blooms, and 'Imperial Crimson' both produce beautiful, fragrant, sideways-facing blooms up to 10 inches (25cm) across on 5-foot (1.5m) stems that will need staking. A bit smaller-flowered than the 'Imperials', but lower in maintenance, is the amazing 'Star Gazer' Oriental lily. Nominated to the North American Lily Hall of Fame, 'Star Gazer' has rich red flowers, a vigorous constitution, and the ability to multiply freely.

Another famous de Graaff hybrid that deserves space in every perennial border is 'Black Dragon'—a tall, highly fragrant trumpet lily with flowers fully 8 inches (20cm) long. Though pure white in the throat, the outside of the trumpet is maroon. Plants grow 5 to 8 feet (1.5 to 2.4m) tall depending on age, and grow in light shade or full sun, provided the roots are mulched and shaded.

All garden lilies thrive in a humus-rich, well-drained soil, and should be fertilized after flowering so that the bulb can replenish itself to rebloom and multiply. A covering of shredded leaves, pine needles, or even grass clippings will not only help keep the soil cool, but will protect the bulbs through winter. Since deer relish the tender lily shoots, you may need to spray the foliage periodically with an odorless deer repellent. If any of your lilies develop seed pods, it is best to remove them, since seed formation can deplete the bulb.

Lilies are easily divided. Simply dig up the roots and separate the bulblets that have formed around the mother bulb. These bulbs are often composed of scales, with each scale capable of producing a new plant when it is covered with soil. Also, many lilies (Japanese tiger lily, for example) produce black bulbils along the stems that readily sprout when they come in contact with soil.

Lobelia cardinalis
(c a r d i n a l   f l o w e r)

Dramatic spires of cardinal flowers are here grown among cattails. Both bloom in midsummer and tolerate permanently moist, swampy soil.

Native to stream banks throughout eastern North America, cardinal flowers produce colonies of tall, erect plants topped with spires of crimson butterfly-shaped florets that are highly attractive to hummingbirds. Though cardinal flowers prefer full sun, they tolerate light shade. They're quite happy in boggy soil, surviving even when the roots are permanently covered with shallow water. Plants grow to 4 feet (1.2m) tall.

There is a wonderful hybrid, called 'Queen Victoria', between this hardy North American species and a tender Mexican species *(L. fulgens)*. 'Queen Victoria' exhibits extra-long flower spikes and rich bronze foliage. It fares well in the Pacific Northwest and other places with mild winters, but is a little too tender for most northern gardens.

Cardinal flowers are easily raised from seed, sown into a peat-based potting soil. They may also be propagated by division after flowering. A related species, *L. syphilitica*, has blue flowers and a more compact, spreading habit (3 feet [90cm] tall). Both are excellent for boggy areas like stream banks and pond margins, especially in combination with hardy hibiscus.

Spires of pink and blue lupines contrast well with red sweet William in a late spring show.

Lupinus species *and* hybrids

(lupines)

Wild lupines are native to North America. Flowers are usually blue or yellow, with attractive leaf clusters composed of slender leaflets arranged in a palm shape. The Carolina yellow lupine *(L. perennis)* makes a strong accent in sunny perennial borders, while the blue Pacific coast lupine, *L. polyphyllus*, has naturalized successfully in coastal and high elevation areas of the Northeast, such as Maine and Long Island, where it thrives in sandy soils. However, none of the wild species can match the spectacular show and color range of the legendary 'Russell Lupines', which were hybridized early this century by George Russell, an English railroad worker, using North American species.

Russell hybrid lupines, which flower mainly in spring, come in white, cream, yellow, pink, red, blue, and purple, as well as many bicolor combinations. They form bushy plants and tall, erect flower spikes studded with pealike flowers that have a pleasant, peppery aroma. Though not long-lived as perennials, they will self-sow and establish generous colonies, especially in meadow gardens. However, plants from seed are generally variable; only by dividing can you propagate the best colors. Lupines prefer full sun and a fertile, well-drained soil. Plants grow to 4 feet (1.2m) tall, though there are several good dwarf types, such as 'Minarette' and 'Lulu.'

Yellow loosestrife mingles its flowers with Japanese maple leaves.

Lysimachia punctata

(garden loosestrife, yellow loosestrife)

This old-fashioned perennial produces incredibly clear yellow flowers in late spring and early summer, at a time when yellow flowers are needed to harmonize with the preponderance of blues. Yellow loosestrife likes full sun and tolerates both dry and boggy soil, surviving in situations where other plants will perish from neglect.

Propagate yellow loosestrife by division. It looks particularly lovely in combination with blue veronicas and blue sages, or it can be planted among dwarf blue spruces.

Lythrum virgatum 'Morden's Pink'

(purple loosestrife)

Though wild purple loosestrife presents problems because of its ability to completely take over certain kinds of wetlands habitats, the variety 'Morden's Pink' is a superb perennial for home gardens. Sometimes listed as *L. salicaria*, but more probably a hybrid, 'Morden's Pink' grows bushy to 4 feet (1.2m) tall, producing erect flower stems loaded with purplish pink flowers that begin to bloom in early summer.

Plant 'Morden's Pink' in full sun in fertile soil (which can be either moist or dry) and keep faded flower spikes deadheaded. Purple loosestrife is a good companion for 'Stella d'Oro' daylily, hardy hybrid hibiscus, perennial sunflowers, cardinal flowers, and cattails. Propagate 3-year clumps by division.

Above left: *Lythrum virgatum* **'Morden's Pink' with gloriosa daisies. Below: 'Strictus' Japanese silver grass resembles a shower of sparks.**

Miscanthus sinensis

(Japanese silver grass, eulalia grass)

There are undoubtedly more varieties of Japanese silver grass than any other ornamental grass. Characterized by long, slender, arching leaf blades in summer and silvery or red flower plumes in autumn, this lovely grass grows up to 6 feet (1.8m) tall, depending on the variety. The narrow leaves can be plain or variegated (both horizontally and vertically). The variety *'Strictus'* (porcupine grass) is a particularly fine variegated form because the green leaves are banded with gold, so the effect of a healthy clump is reminiscent of a shower of sparks! The cultivar 'Variegatus' (variegated Japanese silver grass) is most useful as a background or an accent in perennial gardens, as the silvery sheen of the green and white striped leaves complements many perennial flower colors, particularly yellows, reds, and blues.

Another fine cultivar, 'Purpurascens', is also a great favorite at Cedaridge Farm, since its foliage turns a lovely purple in autumn, remaining ornamental until a hard freeze. Plants thrive in a wide range of soils, from moist to dry, and are content even in impoverished soil. About their only requirement is full sun. They are easily propagated by division.

Japanese silver grasses are the mainstays of ornamental grass gardens, where different shapes, sizes, and textures of grasses are combined in a spectacular yet understated show of elegance.

Monarda didyma

(bee balm)

'Cambridge Scarlet' bee balm makes a strong impact in sun or light shade.

Native to North America, bee balm grows in vigorous clumps of mintlike, fragrant leaves topped by a crown of tubular flowers. The blooms, which range in color from white, red, and pink to purple and burgundy, are highly attractive to bees, hummingbirds, and butterflies. Most varieties bloom for several weeks in midsummer, but 'Cambridge Scarlet' will bloom earlier and longer, lasting up to 6 weeks.

Plants grow to 4 feet (1.2m) tall, and prefer full sun and good drainage. They are best used sparingly as accents; intersperse them among clumps of ornamental grasses, black-eyed Susans, perennial sunflowers, and purple coneflowers.

Nymphaea hybrids
(water lilies)

'Caroliniana Rosea' is a free-flowering, soft pink water lily.

Summer is a great time to evaluate water lilies. Many hardy kinds bloom prolifically from June through September, while the tropicals will continue blooming until a hard frost because of their more robust constitution. You do not need a pond to grow hardy water lilies. Almost all will thrive on a terrace or patio in a tub the size of a whiskey barrel. At Cedaridge Farm we are fortunate enough to have a small pond where we can emulate Claude Monet, the Impressionist painter who collected water lilies as a hobby and celebrated them in dozens of paintings.

An amazing fact is that the varieties Monet collected are among the best-selling varieties today. These hybrids are the result of an aggressive breeding program by a French hybridizer, Joseph Bory Latour Marliac, at his nursery in the south of France, near Bordeaux. In the summer of 1994 I visited the old nursery, stayed overnight in one of Marliac's houses, and photographed many of the forty varieties Monet had purchased.

Marliac started his endeavor by first collecting water lily species from all over the world: *Nymphaea alba* (the European water lily), *N. odorata* (a fragrant white from North America and a pink form found on Cape Cod), and *N. mexicana* (a yellow from Mexico). There was no red when Marliac started, but he found a deep pink in Swedish lakes that turned red with age.

Known botanically as *Nymphaea × marliaca*, some of Marliac's best varieties for North America include 'Caroliniana Rosea' (a lovely clear pink), 'Escarboucle' (a rich carmine-red), 'Comanche' (a glowing orange), 'Chromatella' (a sulphur yellow), and 'Marliaca Albida' (a large, fragrant white).

Whether you want to grow water lilies in tubs or ponds, plant the roots in 3-gallon (11.3L) pots and sink the pots 1 to 2 feet (30 to 60cm) below the surface of the water. Otherwise, the roots can become aggressive and cover the entire pond, which is far less desirable than having compact islands of foliage with reflective water between them. The soil should be a fertile clay loam with garden compost or well-decomposed animal manure mixed in. Water lilies are heavy feeders, and benefit from having fertilizer tablets (usually two at a time) pushed into the soil around their roots, once a month from May until the end of August.

Hardy water lilies will survive freezing winters as long as the pots remain below the ice line. If they are in danger of being frozen by ice, move the pots to deeper water for winter. Even hardy water lilies won't do well in a fast-running stream or where the water temperature does not rise above 70°F (21°C), such as in spring-fed ponds, for most of the summer. Water lilies are excellent companions for pond-side plants such as blue Japanese irises, yellow flag irises, red cardinal flowers, and pink or red astilbes.

Oenothera species

(evening primroses, sundrops)

Low, spreading, pink evening primroses in company with violet sage and blue oat grass create a cool, pink-and-blue color harmony.

Native to North America, both the yellow-flowered *Oenothera tetragona* (commonly called sundrops) and *O. speciosa* (called pink evening primrose) will bloom for 6 weeks. They are low-growing, spreading plants (just 12 inches [30cm] high), and they each deserve space in even the smallest perennial garden, since their cup-shaped shimmering blossoms really light up the landscape.

Plants demand full sun and good drainage. They are excellent for edging beds and borders, and for massing in rock gardens and meadow gardens. *O. tetragona* is sometimes known as *O. fruticosa*. The variety 'Fireworks' has prominent, reddish stems and makes a good companion to dwarf red and yellow Indian blanket, red goatsbeard, and silver mound. *O. speciosa* looks exquisite when planted among blue sages and blue oat grasses.

Paeonia species *and* hybrids
(peonies)

A single 'Barrington Belle' peony plant has close to a hundred red blossoms all open at the same time. Herbaceous peonies can last for a century or longer if left in the same spot.

Most modern varieties of hybrid peonies were developed by breeders in France, England, and North America, using mostly *P. lactiflora* from China and *P. officinalis* from southern Europe. Foremost among American breeders is the Klehm family, of Barrington, Illinois. Their introductions are collectively known as 'Estate Peonies', my favorite of which is 'Barrington Belle', a 4-foot (1.2m)-tall plant that can have a hundred or more bright red, crested, yellow-flecked flowers all open at one time. A good, old-fashioned favorite at Cedaridge Farm is a 1906 French introduction, 'Sarah Bernhardt'. In the second season after planting bareroots we have counted thirty-six blossoms on one plant. The clear pink blooms are exquisite, resembling giant scoops of ice cream. Visitors also admire 'Bowl of Beauty', a cup-shaped, rose pink, single-flowered variety with a prominent dome of yellow stamens.

Though peonies are often sold in 1-gallon (3.7L) and 3-gallon (11.3L) containers for spring planting, it's much less expensive to purchase bareroot divisions for planting in autumn. If you plant them during the cool months of autumn, the tops will remain dormant but the roots will continue to grow through the winter. By spring the roots will be able to support vigorous top growth and resist dehydration from hot, dry summers, which often kills bareroot divisions planted in spring. For best results, peony divisions should have three to five growing points visible.

Peonies are heavy feeders and do best in well-drained soil in a sunny or lightly shaded location. Top-dress the soil with compost in spring before the plants bloom and

in autumn after frost, or fertilize with a granular fertilizer high in phosphorus. Peonies need sharp winters to encourage a period of dormancy, which is essential for long life (established clumps of herbaceous peonies can live for a hundred years or longer).

Peonies are good companions for blue and pink bearded irises, pink and red Oriental poppies, purple foxgloves, and pink bleeding hearts.

Tree peonies are rich in the rose pink color range and thrive in sun or light shade. They grow further south than herbaceous peonies, and some flowers can reach 12 inches (30cm) in diameter.

Paeonia suffruticosa
(tree peonies)

These shrubby plants are larger-flowered (with blooms up to 12 inches [30cm] across) and earlier-flowering than herbaceous peonies. Also, tree peonies don't need as cold a dormancy period as herbaceous peonies, allowing them to be grown further south. Essential are a humus-rich, fertile soil and roots sheltered from prevailing winds (preferably by a low stone wall). The most coveted of all tree peonies is 'Rock's Variety', a huge, white, semidouble, ruffled variety with maroon markings that was propagated from a single plant discovered in a Chinese monastery during a plant-finding expedition financed by the National Geographic Society. Some of the best tree peony hybrids (especially among yellows—a color absent from herbaceous peonies) are the result of work by a New York hybridist, the late Dr. A.P. Saunders. 'Gold Sovereign' (a semidouble yellow) and 'Harvest' (a semidouble apricot-colored variety with a flower form like a giant camellia) are especially beautiful.

Papaver orientale

(Oriental poppy)

Of all the flowers celebrated in art and literature, none seems to please people more than the poppy. An analysis of Impressionist art, for example, shows more paintings of poppies than roses, irises, or sunflowers. Though many poppies are annuals (such as the Shirley poppy and the California poppy), many are perennials, including the large-flowered *P. orientale* and the even larger flowered *P. bracteatum* (Himalayan poppy, sometimes listed as *P. orientale bracteatum*).

Though neither are long-lasting in bloom (flowering for a week to 10 days at the most), individual flowers can measure up to 10 inches (25cm) across. Simple to grow from seed (with blooms appearing the second season), they are even more easily grown from root cuttings. The seed is dustlike and needs to be sown on the surface of a peat-based potting soil. The seeds must be kept moist by misting, and the resulting seedlings should be transferred to individual peat pots until they reach transplant size (a plant diameter of 4 inches [10cm] across). To raise Oriental poppies from root cuttings, simply dig up a clump of roots and, with a sharp knife, cut the fleshy roots into 1-inch (2.5cm) segments. Cover the segments with soil and water; each segment will contain a tiny growing scar and from this scar will grow roots and leaves. Oriental poppies are extremely hardy, and after they flower it is natural for them to go dormant during summer heat. The leafy crown should grow back as soon as cool weather returns, and this green crown survives even severe winters to bloom again in spring. Once transplanted, Oriental poppies resent any kind of root disturbance. Some of my favorite varieties include the pink 'Helen Elizabeth' and the crimson 'Beauty of Livermore'. All are enhanced by decorative seed pods and a powdery crown of black stamens.

Oriental poppies demand full sun and prefer a sheltered position to protect them from wind damage. Colors include white, pink, red, and purple as well as several bicolors—some with black splashed at the base of each petal. The satinlike petals have a silky sheen, and the flowers are perfect companions to herbaceous peonies, bearded irises, and late-flowering tulips. The variety 'Allegro' is a special, compact, dwarf type that resists wind damage.

Other cheerful perennial poppies include the Iceland poppy *(P. nudicaule)* and the alpine poppy *(P. alpinum)*. Both are early-flowering and predominate in white, yellow, orange, apricot, and pink. Iceland poppies are not as long-lived as the alpines, but bear larger flowers.

These red Oriental poppies—planted with irises, peonies, climbing roses, and billowing pink tamarix—are an awe-inspiring addition to the garden of Impressionist painter Claude Monet.

Phlox
species
(p h l o x)

Most species of phlox seen in North American gardens—including *P. divaricata* (wild blue phlox), *P. maculata* (Carolina phlox), *P. subulata* (creeping phlox) and *P. paniculata* (summer phlox)—are native to North America. All of these deserve space in perennial gardens.

Wild blue phlox is an extremely desirable plant for shade gardens. It flowers in early spring, at the same time as tulips, and is capable of creating generous colonies. There is also a creeping form of wild blue phlox *(P. stolonifera)* which makes a superb groundcover. Both grow just 8 inches (20cm) tall.

Carolina phlox looks exactly like summer phlox, but it blooms several weeks earlier and is not as susceptible to mildew. At 3 feet (90cm) tall, it's a bit shorter and is generally more vigorous, creating a greater density of color. The varieties 'Alpha' (pink) and 'Omega' (white with a red eye) are superb plants, blooming for up to 6 weeks. They are wonderful companions to daylilies, garden lilies, and shrub roses.

Creeping phlox flowers early, at the same time as daffodils and early tulips. In mild climates, the foliage is evergreen. Though the most common varieties are red, pink, white, and blue, there are some interesting bicolors. Just 4 inches (10cm) tall, creeping phlox likes a sunny exposure and well-drained soil. It is at its best planted as a flowering carpet on sunny slopes or as drifts in rock gardens.

Summer phlox are tall and upright, with huge flower clusters in white, pink,

'Alpha' Carolina phlox is a vibrant rose pink and blooms several weeks earlier than summer phlox.

red, and lavender-blue, many with contrasting red eyes. Unfortunately, most are susceptible to mildew disease, which is controlled only by spraying young plants at intervals with a fungicide. However, the variety 'Eva Cullum' (pink with a red eye) is not only mildew resistant but capable of 12 weeks of nonstop bloom. Summer phlox are good companions for false sunflowers and black-eyed Susans, though these 5-foot (1.5m)-tall plants invariably need staking to keep them erect. They are easily propagated by division and root cuttings.

Primula species *and* hybrids
(p r i m r o s e s)

Few people realize that, although the primrose has strong associations with England, the finest strain of primroses the world has ever seen was developed by an impoverished American concert pianist, Florence Levy, in Portland, Oregon. Over a period of forty years she produced the famous 'Barnhaven' strain of primroses, introducing not only new colors, such as blue and pink, but also double-flowered and lace-edged kinds. Using the 'Barnhavens' as parents, a California plant breeder produced the large-flowered 'Pacific Giants' strain of *P. × polyantha*. These are the primroses most commonly offered in bloom by nurseries in spring. Though the range of colors is extensive and flower size impressive, 'Pacific Giants' do not have the old-fashioned charm of the 'Barnhavens'.

The sad fact is that with the enormous popularity of the 'Pacific Giants' strain, the 'Barnhaven' strain is becoming harder and harder to find. When Mrs. Levy retired she entrusted her stocks to the owners of a British nursery, and when they in turn retired, the stocks were entrusted to a nursery in Brittany, France. The loveliest of 'Barnhaven' primroses—the laced-edged cultivars—are available from seed through Thompson & Morgan (see Sources [page 116]). Primroses don't fare well in very warm climates, but I feel strongly that all home gardens in temperate areas should have a patch of 'Barnhaven' primroses.

To grow primroses from seed, scatter them onto a bed of peat-based potting soil. Primrose seeds are tiny and can dry out quickly, so mist the soil surface to keep it moist. A plastic bag around the seed tray will hasten germination. Once the seedlings are up they should be transferred to individual pots; transfer them to the garden once they have produced a healthy rosette of leaves 4 inches (10cm) across. Primroses may also be divided after flowering. The plants prefer light shade and a humus-rich soil. They will grow in full sun, provided the soil is kept cool by irrigation and an organic mulch.

The old-fashioned Barnhaven primrose cultivar 'Gold Lace' has gleaming yellow centers and distinctive black petals edged with yellow.

Primroses are excellent companions to bluebells, purple honesty, blue woodland phlox, pink bleeding hearts, and white foamflower.

Another group of perennial primroses is known as the candelabras. These include *Primula japonica* (by far the hardiest for northern gardens) in white, pink, red, and purple, and *Primula beesiana*, which predominates in yellows and orange. Candelabras like boggy, humus-rich soils, and fare especially well along the edges of streams. They produce rosettes of crinkly green leaves and erect flower stems up to 2 feet (60cm) tall, with flowers arranged in whorls. Both kinds are wonderful companions to blue-leafed hostas and blue Siberian irises.

The black-eyed Susan 'Goldsturm' displays a truly amazing quantity of bright yellow flowers.

Rudbeckia fulgida

(black-eyed Susan)

Black-eyed Susans (also known as *R. hirta*) sport yellow, daisylike flowers with black buttonlike centers. Native to North America, they thrive in open meadows and along roadsides, even in impoverished soil. Two major plant breeding innovations have turned the wildling into a superb display flower for home gardens: first, the introduction of large-flowered annual kinds (called gloriosa daisies), which are actually perennials that will bloom the first year from seed; second, the introduction of a sterile variety, 'Goldsturm', which will not set viable seed and which puts all its energy into producing an extraordinary number of flowers. Unfortunately, some nurseries try to take advantage of the reputation of the 'Goldsturm' name and sell plants raised from seeds, but for the originator's variety plants must be grown from divisions. When buying 'Goldsturm' always ask if it has been seed-raised or divided. Plants grow to 4 feet (1.2m) tall.

A particularly fine strain of gloriosa daisy is 'Irish Eyes'. The button center of the flower is green rather than black. Best raised from seed, which can be sown directly into the garden onto bare soil as early in spring as the soil can be worked, plants grow quickly and flower by midsummer. If the flowering display starts to diminish, the plants can be cut back to the ground to produce another flush of flowers.

Rudbeckias demand full sun and good drainage for best results. They are excellent companions to ornamental grasses, red bee balm, pink stonecrop, red daylilies, and yellow perennial sunflowers. Use rudbeckias in mixed borders or in meadow gardens, especially in combination with purple coneflowers.

Salvia × superba
(violet sage)

'May Night' violet sage partnered with 'Johnson's Blue' geranium creates a striking monochromatic scheme in late spring.

Blue sage, also known as *S. nemerosa*, forms beautiful, bushy, spreading clumps of spear-shaped, aromatic leaves and conspicuous, erect flower spikes in various shades of blue. Older varieties like 'East Friesland' are usually violet-blue, while some varieties, such as 'Lubeca', produce a truer blue, and others, like 'May Night', are deep blue. These newer varieties will bloom for 12 weeks starting in June if the first flush of flowers is cut back when they start to fade.

Plants grow to 2 feet (60cm) tall and flower spectacularly in full sun and a well-drained soil. Use them in mixed borders, especially with yellow varieties of yarrow, loosestrife, and foxgloves.

Scabiosa columbaria
(pincushion flower)

Most people are familiar with *S. caucasica*, the 2½-foot (75cm)-tall blue pincushion flower that has been around for generations. It is valued for cutting, and for early-summer displays when it contrasts beautifully with yellow coreopsis. However, not many gardeners are yet familiar with the more compact *S. columbaria*. Two new varieties, 'Butterfly Blue' and 'Pink Mist', form bushy clumps just 15 inches (38cm) tall, loaded with blue or pink flowers for up to 18 weeks, from early spring to autumn frost.

Plants thrive in full sun and will tolerate poor soil provided drainage is good. Mass them in mixed beds and borders or use them as edging plants. Propagate pincushion flowers by division.

'Butterfly Blue' is an everblooming variety of pincushion flower that blooms freely for 18 months and is highly attractive to butterflies.

Sedum
spectabile
and hybrids
(stonecrops)

One of the finest attractions for butterflies (especially monarchs and swallowtails), stonecrops are blue-green succulents that for most of the summer look like heads of broccoli, then erupt into a dense display of flat flower clusters that remain colorful for several weeks. The variety 'Brilliancy' has extra-large flower heads and a dazzling, rosy pink hue that sets it apart from other varieties. However, a much longer lasting stonecrop is 'Autumn Joy', a hybrid that starts off deep pink, turns red at maturity, then deepens to cinnamon as the flower heads dry. As a consequence, 'Autumn Joy' remains colorful for 10 weeks or more—until heavy snows or ice shatter the dried stems.

Both 'Brilliancy' and 'Autumn Joy' are excellent companions for ornamental grasses. They are drought-tolerant, prefer full sun, and tolerate poor soil provided drainage is good. The plants are easily divided, and can also be propagated from stem or leaf cuttings. Plants grow to 2 feet (60cm) tall.

Stonecrops are a large perennial plant family, and many other forms, notably the red-flowering *S. spurium* ('Dragons Blood' sedum) and yellow flowering *S. kamtschaticum*, are excellent for edging mixed perennial borders or for creating carpeting effects in rock gardens.

Above: 'Autumn Joy' stonecrop mixes with miscanthus grass and New England asters in a lovely autumn border. Below: A flowering clump of silvery lamb's ears.

Stachys olympica
(lamb's ears)

One of the perennial kingdom's finest foliage plants, lamb's ears forms ground-hugging, evergreen rosettes of woolly, silvery leaves the shape of a lamb's ear. Though erect woolly flower spikes with inconspicuous pink flowers appear in midsummer, the plant's true value lies in its ability to bind together color elements in the garden. Though many other perennials produce good silvery accents (such as *Cineraria maritima* and *Artemisia* species), lamb's ears, also known as *S. byzantina*, is special because of its low, spreading habit.

The variety 'Silver Carpet' is a sterile hybrid that develops no flower spikes, making it especially good for groundcover effects. 'Helene Von Stein' has extra-large leaves and flowers rarely. Plants prefer full sun and a fertile, well-drained soil, though 'Helene Von Stein' will tolerate moist soils that can rot other varieties.

Propagate lamb's ears by division. Use it as an edging plant, or mix it with pink, red, and blue perennials to sharpen these colors.

Veronica species

(speedwells)

Veronica alpina 'Goodness Grows' looks spectacular when mixed with a multitude of red and pink astilbes.

Native to Europe, the best speedwells are bushy, clump-forming plants 15 inches (38cm) tall. They are valued for prodigious quantities of blue flower spikes, although pink and white varieties are also available. Two varieties in particular are outstanding as everblooming perennials. *V. alpina* 'Goodness Grows', cultivated from a chance seedling that appeared in a Georgia nursery of the same name, spreads to 2 feet (60cm) wide, with lovely violet-blue flowers that last for 14 weeks. 'Sunny Border Blue', believed to be a hybrid of *V. longifolia*, was discovered at Sunny Border Nurseries in Connecticut. Growing to 2 feet (60cm) tall, the flower spikes are a deep blue and last for 14 weeks as well.

Resembling blue sages, these veronicas like full sun and a fertile, well-drained soil. Use them with orange and yellow-flowering perennials, such as red-hot pokers, coreopsis, and 'Stella d'Oro' daylilies.

Yucca filamentosa

(Adam's needle, needle palm)

Drought-tolerant flowering yucca and hardy prickly pear cactus.

Native to North America, though various forms of yucca can be found from Canada to Mexico and from coast to coast, it's difficult to believe that these evergreen plants are hardy perennials rather than tender desert plants. The spiky, sword-shaped leaves look as though they come from a Caribbean island, and the immense white flower plumes (up to 6 feet [1.8m] tall) are exotic. Of particular interest is the variegated 'Golden Sword', which has yellow-edged leaves. This makes a wonderful accent in mixed borders, staying 2 feet (60cm) high until flowering occurs (usually in the third or fourth season) when a flower spike resembling a giant asparagus spear towers to 5 feet (1.5m) high and opens out into a dazzling white candelabra of blossoms.

These drought-tolerant plants demand full sun but tolerate any kind of soil that has good drainage. They are excellent for covering sunny slopes and for massing in colonies, especially with attractive ornamental grasses such as golden carex and blue fescues. Yuccas are also good companions for other succulents such as stonecrops, hens and chickens, and hardy prickly-pear. The flowers are slightly fragrant and edible, tasting like lettuce. Propagate by division.

About
the
Author

Derek Fell is a writer and photographer who specializes in gardening, with an emphasis on step-by-step gardening concepts and garden design. He lives in Bucks County, Pennsylvania, at historic Cedaridge Farm, Tinicum Township, where he cultivates extensive award-winning flower and vegetable gardens that have been featured in *Architectural Digest, Garden Design, Beautiful Gardens, Gardens Illustrated, American Nurseryman,* and *Mid-Atlantic Country* magazines. Born and educated in England, he first worked for seven years with Europe's largest seed company, then moved to Pennsylvania in 1964 to work for Burpee Seeds as their catalog manager, a position he held for six years before taking on duties as executive director of the All-America Selections (the national seed trials) and the National Garden Bureau (an information office sponsored by the American seed industry). Now the author of more than fifty garden books and calendars, he has traveled widely throughout North America, also documenting gardens in Europe, Africa, New Zealand, and Asia. His most recent books are *Renoir's Garden* (Simon & Schuster), *The Impressionist Garden* (Crown), *500 Perennial Garden Ideas* (Simon & Schuster), and *In the Garden with Derek* (Camino Books).

A frequent contributor to *Architectural Digest* and *Woman's Day* magazines, Derek Fell is the winner of more awards from the Garden Writers Association of America than any other garden writer. He also worked as a consultant on gardening to the White House during the Ford Administration.

Wall calendars, greeting cards, and art posters featuring Derek Fell's photography are published worldwide. He has lectured on photography and the gardens of the great Impressionist painters at numerous art museums, including the Smithsonian Institution in Washington, D.C.; the Philadelphia Museum of Art, the Barnes Foundation, Philadelphia; and the Denver Art Museum, Colorado. He is also host of a regular garden show for the QVC cable television shopping channel, entitled *Step-by-Step Gardening,* which is plugged into fifty million homes.

Fell's highly acclaimed *Step-by-Step Gardening* mail-order perennial plant catalogs for Spring Hill Nurseries (North America's largest mail-order nursery) reach an audience of home gardeners estimated to be more than three million in spring and autumn. He is a former president of the Hobby Greenhouse Association, a former director of the Garden Writers Association of America, the president of the International Test Gardeners Association, and a cofounder of the American Gardening Association.

A complete list of published works follows.

Books by Derek Fell

(asterisk indicates coauthorship)

The White House Vegetable Garden. 1976, Exposition.

House Plants for Fun & Profit. 1978, Bookworm.

How to Photograph Flowers, Plants, & Landscapes. 1980, HP Books.

Vegetables: How to Select, Grow, and Enjoy. 1982, HP Books.

Annuals: How to Select, Grow, and Enjoy. 1983, HP Books.

Deerfield: An American Garden Through Four Seasons. 1986, Pidcock Press.

Trees & Shrubs. 1986, HP Books.

Garden Accents. 1987, Henry Holt (*Inspired Garden* in the United Kingdom).

*Discover Anguilla. 1988, Caribbean Concepts.

*Home Landscaping. 1988, Simon & Schuster.

The One-Minute Gardener. 1988, Running Press.

A Kid's First Gardening Book. 1989, Running Press.

*Three Year Garden Journal. 1989, Starwood.

*Ornamental Grass Gardening. 1989, HP Books.

*The Complete Garden Planning Manual. 1989, HP Books.

The Essential Gardener. 1990, Crown.

Essential Roses. 1990, Crown.

Essential Annuals. 1990, Crown.

Essential Bulbs. 1990, Crown.

Essential Herbs. 1990, Crown.

Essential Perennials. 1990, Crown.

Essential Shrubs. 1990, Crown.

The Easiest Flower to Grow. 1990, Ortho.

*550 Home Landscaping Ideas. 1991, Simon & Schuster.

Renoir's Garden. 1991, Simon & Schuster.

Beautiful Bucks County. 1991, Cedaridge.

* The Encyclopedia of Ornamental Grasses. 1992, Smithmark.

The Encyclopedia of Flowers. 1993, Smithmark.

Garden Guide: Annuals. 1993, Smithmark.

Garden Guide: Perennials. 1993, Smithmark.

Garden Guide: Bulbs. 1993, Smithmark.

Garden Guide: Roses. 1993, Smithmark.

*550 Perennial Garden Ideas. 1993, Simon & Schuster.

The Impressionist Garden. 1994, Crown.

*Practical Gardening. 1995, Friedman/Fairfax.

*Gardens of Philadelphia & the Delaware Valley. 1995, Temple University Press.

The Pennsylvania Gardener. 1995, Camino Books.

In the Garden with Derek. 1995, Camino Books.

Calendars

Great Gardens (Portal)

The Impressionist Garden (Portal)

The Gardening Year (Portal)

Perennials (Starwood)

Flowering Shrubs (Starwood)

Flowering Bulbs (Starwood)

Northeast Gardens Calendar (Starwood)

Mid-Atlantic Gardens Calendar (Starwood)

Southern Gardens Calendar (Starwood)

California Gardens Calendar (Starwood)

Pacific Northwest Gardens Calendar (Starwood)

Art Posters

Deerfield Garden (Portal)

Spring Garden (Portal)

Monet's Bridge (Portal)

Sources

Following is a list of suppliers of perennials. Some are specialists in a particular plant group. Note that some of the catalogs are free; others require a small charge. Those who are not mail-order suppliers have extensive production fields and/or display gardens where rare and unusual varieties can be obtained, and are well worth a visit.

**Andre Viette Farm
and Nursery**
Route 1, Box 16
Fisherville, VA 22939

This colorful catalog features a connoisseur's selection of perennials. Catalog: $2.00.

B&D Lilies
330 P Street
Port Townsend, WA
98368

An excellent catalog loaded with detailed descriptions and growing advice. Full-color catalog: $1.00.

Bluestone Perennials
7211 Middle Ridge Road
Madison, OH 44057

This colorful catalog features an excellent selection of old and new varieties. Catalog: free.

Busse Gardens
Route 2, Box 238
Cokato, MN 55321

Extensive listing of popular perennials. Strong listings of goatsbeard, heartleaf, geraniums, and peonies. Black-and-white catalog: $2.00.

**Chehalis Rare
Plant Nursery**
2568 Jackson Highway
Chehalis, WA 98532

Specialists in primroses, offering only seed by mail. Send a self-addressed stamped envelope for list. Plants sold at the nursery.

Cooley's Gardens
11553 Silverton Road NE
Silverton, OR 97381

More than two hundred acres (80ha) of bearded irises under cultivation, plus new hybrids. Full-color catalog: $2.00.

Daylily Discounters
1 Daylily Plaza
Alachua, FL 32615

Beautiful full-color catalog. Display gardens and production fields open to the public in season. Catalog: free.

Far North Gardens
16785 Harrison
Livonia, MI 48154

Plants and seeds of the famous and now hard-to-find 'Barnhaven' primroses. Black-and-white catalog: $2.00.

Fleming's Flower Fields
3100 Leighton Avenue
Box 4617
Lincoln, NE 68504

Specialists in chrysanthemums. Black-and-white catalog: free.

Klehm Nursery
Box 197
South Barrington, IL
60010

The catalog features both herbaceous peonies (including the world famous 'Estate' line) and tree peonies plus extensive listings of daylilies and hostas. Full-color catalog: $2.00.

Kurt Bluemel Inc.
2740 Green Lane
Baldwin, MD 31013

Black-and-white catalog filled with excellent descriptions and sensitive line drawings of not only grasses, but grass look-alikes such as rushes and sedges. Catalog: $2.00.

Lee Bristol Nursery
Route 55, Box 5
Gaylordsville, CT 06755

Broad selection of daylilies listed by color. Nursery and gardens open to the public. Catalog: free.

Lilypons Water Gardens
6338 Lilypons Road
Lilypons, MD 21717

Handsome catalog features an extensive selection of hardy and tropical waterlilies, aquatic plants, and bog plants, plus fish and supplies. Full-color catalog: $3.50.

Niche Gardens
1111 Dawson Road
Chapel Hill, NC 27516

Excellent selection of perennials, including pink cardinal flowers and hardy pitcher plants. Black-and-white catalog: $3.00.

Piccadilly Farm
1971 Whippoorwill Road
Bishop, GA 30621

Plant list of hostas and also hellebores, all very reasonably priced. Black-and-white plant list: free.

Plants of the Southwest
930 Baca Street
Santa Fe, NM 87501

Colorful catalog featuring many drought-tolerant perennial plants indigenous to the Southwest. Catalog: free.

Rex Bulb Farms
2569 Washington Street
Port Townsend, WA
98368

Features both hybrids and species. Full-color catalog: $1.00.

Shreiner's Gardens
3625 Qinaby Road NE
Salem, OR 97303

Bearded irises including many award winners. Full-color catalog: $2.00.

Siskyou Rare
Plant Nursery
2825 Cummings Road
Medford, OR 97501

Fine selection of hard-to-find perennials, particularly alpines and rock garden plants such as primroses.

Slocum Water Gardens
1101 Cypress Gardens
Boulevard
Winter Haven, FL 33880

Specialists in waterlilies and lotuses. Beautiful display garden. Catalog: $2.00.

Van Ness Water Gardens
2460 North Euclid
Upland, CA 91786

Colorful catalog offers everything for the water gardener. Beautiful display gardens feature sample plantings that are easily adapted to a small scale. Catalog: $2.00.

Walters Gardens
Box 127
Zeeland, MI 49464

Colorful catalog features all the best perennial plant varieties, with a heavy emphasis on hostas.

Wayside Gardens
Garden Lane
Hodges, SC 29695

North America's most colorful and most enticing perennial plant catalog. Catalog: free.

Western Hills Rare
Plant Nursery
16250 Coleman Valley
Road
Occidental, CA 95465

California's finest source for perennials. Though the company does no mail-order business, its display garden is a gem.

White Flower Farm
Route 63
Litchfield, CT 06759

Full-color catalog features a fine selection of hardy perennials, with a strong emphasis on garden lilies. Display gardens and production fields are well worth visiting. Catalog: free.

Wild, Gilbert H. & Son
1112 Joplin Street
Sarcoxie, MO 64862

Catalog features mostly herbaceous peonies and daylilies. Full-color catalog: $2.00.

*Canadian
Sources*

Ferncliff Gardens
SS 1
Mission, British Columbia
V2V 5V6

Specializes in irise and peonies.

McFayden Seed Co. Ltd.
Box 1800
Brandon, Manitoba
R7A 6N4

Seeds and perennial plants.

Stirling Perennials
RR 1
Morpeth, Ontario
N0P 1X0

Full selection of hardy perennials.

Index